THE COMPLETE DIA UK COOKBOOK FOR THE NEWLY DIAGNOSED

1500 Days of Simple and Delicious Recipes for Balanced Meals and Healthy Lifestyle With the Complete Guide to the Diabetic Diet |Full Color Pictures Version

AMELIE HORTON

Table of Contents

Introduction

If you have diabetes or know someone with the condition, this book is for you. It will help you make quick and easy meals that can help you manage your diabetes. Not only can a person with diabetes enjoy these meals, but the entire family can also enjoy them. There are numerous options for gluten-free, low-sodium, and vegan recipes. Additionally, desserts and quick snacks help you manage the condition.

PREVALENCE OF DIABETES

Diabetes is a major issue affecting the UK population. According to the latest figures, over 3.9 million people in the UK live with the condition. There are another 13.6 million people at serious risk of developing diabetes. That makes for a huge segment of the UK population. As such, eating healthy, whether diabetic or pre-diabetic, is a national priority. This cookbook is designed to make a positive contribution to managing the condition.

A HEALTHY DIET MATTERS

Whether you have diabetes or not, a healthy diet matters. However, it is especially so for a family where someone has diabetes. It can be useful in managing weight and preventing conditions like stroke and heart disease.

The recipes are crafted to be wholesome and enjoyable for everyone. If there are kids in the family, these recipes will help them learn, from a young age, that eating healthy can be fun. Later on, it could be useful in helping to prevent adult-onset diabetes or type 2 diabetes. The meals in this cookbook are also great for those that are pre-diabetic. It will ensure that they do not progress to the next stage.

The recipes are designed to be life-long. As such, they are meant to be enjoyed at all times, during all occasions and seasons. The ingredients used are diverse to ensure flavorful meals while also ensuring that users of the cookbook can find ingredients for all seasons.

SIMPLE RECIPES

The recipes in this cookbook are kept simple, with common ingredients available at the local store. You can find the ingredients to help you eat healthily and with ease. These recipes are meant to make it as easy as possible to switch to a diet that caters to your health needs while also pleasing the palate.

While they are easy to make, they are not repetitive. They are designed to make life enjoyable, despite your condition. You do not have to worry about eating 'boring' meals for the rest of your life. With this cookbook, everything can be as fun and exciting as it has always been.

HAVE FUN

The recipes in this cookbook are not set in stone. Have fun mixing them up and creating unique meals for yourself and the family. However, always remember to plan each meal based on how much carbohydrates you should consume. If you dislike your creations, try again until you find a tasty combination.

All recipes in this cookbook limit simple sugars, include fiber, and include healthy protein and fats. Adhering to these principles helps to maintain blood sugar levels within the target ranges.

Chapter 1
Basics of Diabetes and Diabetic diet

What is Diabetes?

Diabetes is a chronic condition that affects the body's ability to produce or use insulin, a hormone that is necessary for regulating blood sugar levels. In people with diabetes, the body either does not produce enough insulin, does not use insulin effectively, or both. As a result, blood sugar levels can become too high, which can cause a range of health problems.

There are two main types of diabetes: type 1 and type 2. In type 1 diabetes, the body does not produce enough insulin, and people with this type of diabetes must take insulin injections to regulate their blood sugar levels. In type 2 diabetes, the body does not use insulin effectively, and people with this type of diabetes may need to take oral medications or insulin injections to manage their blood sugar levels.

Both types of diabetes can be managed through a combination of medication, regular physical activity, and a healthy diet. By following a healthy eating plan and monitoring their blood sugar levels, people with diabetes can reduce their risk of developing diabetes-related complications such as heart disease, nerve damage, and kidney damage.

DIET AND DIABETES

Diet plays a crucial role in managing diabetes because the types and amounts of foods that a person eats can affect their blood sugar levels. Consuming too many foods that are high in sugar and simple carbohydrates can cause large fluctuations in blood sugar levels, which can be harmful for people with diabetes. On the other hand, following a balanced and healthy eating plan can help regulate blood sugar levels and prevent complications.

A diabetic diet is a healthy eating plan that is tailored to a person's individual needs and preferences. It typically includes a variety of fruits, vegetables, whole grains, lean proteins, and healthy fats, and it may exclude or limit certain types of foods that are high in sugar and simple carbohydrates. By following a diabetic diet, people with diabetes can help regulate their blood sugar levels and maintain a healthy weight, which can reduce their risk of developing diabetes-related complications.

In addition to regulating blood sugar levels and controlling weight, a diabetic diet can also provide essential nutrients that support overall health. A healthy eating plan can provide vitamins, minerals, and fiber, which can support immune function, digestive health, and heart health. By following a diabetic diet, people with diabetes can improve their overall health and well-being.

What is the Diabetic Diet?

A diabetic diet is a healthy eating plan that is tailored to a person's individual needs and preferences. It is designed to help people with diabetes regulate their blood sugar levels and prevent complications.

A diabetic diet typically includes a variety of fruits, vegetables, whole grains, lean proteins, and healthy fats. It may exclude or limit certain types of foods that are high in sugar and simple carbohydrates, such as sweets, sugary drinks, and processed foods. By following a diabetic diet, people with diabetes can help regulate their blood sugar levels and maintain a healthy weight, which can reduce their risk of developing diabetes-related complications.

A diabetic diet is not a one-size-fits-all plan, and the specific foods that are included or excluded may vary depending on a person's individual needs and preferences. A healthcare provider can provide individualized guidance on the types and amounts of foods that are best for managing diabetes.

The Components of a Diabetic Diet

THE COMPONENTS OF A DIABETIC DIET ARE:

Fruits: Fruits are a good source of vitamins, minerals, and fiber, and they are generally low in sugar and calories. Fruits that can be included in a diabetic diet include berries, apples, pears, and citrus fruits.

Vegetables: Vegetables are a good source of vitamins, minerals, and fiber, and they are generally low in sugar and calories. Vegetables that can be included in a diabetic diet include leafy greens, broccoli, carrots, and tomatoes.

Whole grains: Whole grains are a good source of fiber, vitamins, and minerals, and they are generally low in sugar and calories. Whole grains that can be included in a diabetic diet include oats, quinoa, barley, and brown rice.

Lean proteins: Lean proteins are a good source of essential amino acids, and they are generally low in saturated fat and calories. Lean proteins that can be included in a diabetic diet include chicken, turkey, fish, tofu, and eggs.

Healthy fats: Healthy fats are a good source of essential fatty acids, and they are generally low in saturated fat and calories. Healthy fats that can be included in a diabetic diet include olive oil, avocado, and nuts.

It is important to note that the specific fruits, vegetables, whole grains, lean proteins, and healthy fats that can be included in a diabetic diet may vary depending on a person's individual needs and preferences. A healthcare provider can provide individualized guidance on the types and amounts of these foods that are best for managing diabetes.

What Foods to Avoid on a Diabetic Diet?

On a diabetic diet, it is generally recommended to avoid foods that are high in sugar and simple carbohydrates. These types of foods can cause large fluctuations in blood sugar levels, which can be harmful for people with diabetes. Some examples of foods that should be avoided on a diabetic diet are:

Sweets and desserts: Cake, cookies, ice cream, and candy

Sugary drinks: Soda, fruit juice, and sports drinks

Processed foods: Frozen meals, packaged snacks, and processed meats

White bread, pasta, and rice: These foods are made with refined grains, which are high in simple carbohydrates

Fried foods: French fries, fried chicken, and donuts

Chapter 2
30 Days Meal Plan

Days	Breakfast	Lunch	Dinner
Day 1	Raspberry Lemonade Smoothies	Cabbage Slaw Salad	Greens Shrimp Salad
Day 2	Peanut Butter S' Mores	Skillet-Blackened Chicken	Hoppin John
Day 3	Tomato Parmesan Mini Quiches	Tuscan Pork Loin	Red Beans
Day 4	Tropical Fruit 'n Ginger Oatmeal	Easy Crab Cakes	Three Bean and Basil Salad
Day 5	Crunchy-Topped Strawberry-Kiwi Parfaits	Beet Greens and Black Beans	Greek Chicken Stuffed Peppers
Day 6	Banana Pancakes	Tuna Egg Salad	Edamame Peanut Bowl
Day 7	Kiwi Salsa with Chips	Beef and Vegetable Soup	Clam Chowder
Day 8	Ham & Jicama Hash	Mexican Zucchini Casserole	Chicken and Egg Noodle Soup
Day 9	Holiday Strata	Eggplant Stew	Rice & Cuban Style Pork
Day 10	Grain Flapjacks	Tuna, Hummus, and Veggie Wraps	Pumpkin White Bean Soup
Day 11	Roasted Veggies with Baked Eggs	Creamy Garlic Chicken with Broccoli	Avocado-Broccoli Soup
Day 12	Tropical Fruit 'n Ginger Oatmeal	Hoppin John	Teriyaki Chicken and Broccoli
Day 13	Corn Cakes & Eggs	Carrot Mushrooms Soup	Avocado Shrimp Salad
Day 14	Ham & Jicama Hash	Green Salmon Florentine	Cheesy Beef & Noodles
Day 15	Triple-Berry Oatmeal Muesli	Mango-Glazed Pork Tenderloin Roast	Avocado-Broccoli Soup
Day 16	Peanut Butter S' Mores	Easy Pad Thai	Roasted Veggies with Flank Steak
Day 17	Holiday Strata	Quick Bison Meatballs	Crust Less Pizza
Day 18	Bacon and Tomato Frittata	Chilled Parsley-Gazpacho	Warm Barley and Squash Salad with Balsamic Vinaigrette
Day 19	Kiwi Salsa with Chips	Corn Shrimp Salad	Crust Less Pizza
Day 20	Hawaiian Breakfast Bake	Tuna and Avocado Salad	Coconut Lime Chicken

Day 21	Italian Breakfast Bake	Easy Pad Thai	Shrimp Olives Salad
Day 22	Raspberry Lemonade Smoothies	Rainbow Black Bean Salad	Chicken and Egg Noodle Soup
Day 23	Hot Maple Porridge	Roasted Veggies with Flank Steak	Tuna Cucumber Salad
Day 24	Creamy Key Lime Pie	Salt-Free Chickpeas	Carrot Millet Soup
Day 25	Banana Pancakes	Stuffed Portobello Mushrooms	Turkey Scaloppini
Day 26	Corn Cakes & Eggs	Avocado-Broccoli Soup	Crab Cakes with Salsa
Day 27	Triple-Berry Oatmeal Muesli	Creamy Braised Oxtails	Eggplant Stew
Day 28	Crunchy-Topped Strawberry-Kiwi Parfaits	Beet Greens and Black Beans	Cabbage Slaw Salad
Day 29	Tomato Parmesan Mini Quiches	Red Beans	Chestnut Stuffed Pork Roast
Day 30	Bacon and Tomato Frittata	Crock Pot Carnitas	Shrimp Cocktail

Chapter 3
Breakfast

Raspberry Lemonade Smoothies

Prep Time: 10 minutes | Cook Time: 10 minutes | Serves 4

- 1 cup refrigerated raspberry lemonade
- 2 ripe bananas, thickly sliced
- 1½ cups fresh raspberries
- 2 containers (6 oz each) raspberry fat-free yogurt

1. In blender or food processor, place all ingredients.
2. Cover | blend on high speed about 1 minute or until smooth and creamy. Pour into glasses. Serve immediately.

PER SERVING

Calories: 190 | Total Fat: 1.5g | Cholesterol: 5mg | Sodium: 45mg | Total Carbs: 42g | Protein: 3g

Crunchy-Topped Strawberry-Kiwi Parfaits

Prep Time: 10 minutes | Cook Time: 20 minutes | Serves 4

- 2 cups Banana Nut Cheerios® cereal
- ¼ cup sliced almonds
- 1½ cups creamy vanilla or creamy peach fat-free yogurt
- 1 cup sliced fresh strawberries
- 2 medium kiwifruit, peeled, cut into chunks

1. Heat oven to 350°F. In ungreased 13x9-inch pan, place cereal and almonds. Bake 6 to 10 minutes, stirring occasionally, until light brown. Cool about 5 minutes.
2. In each of 4 parfait glasses, alternate layers of yogurt, strawberries, kiwifruit and toasted cereal mixture. Serve immediately.

PER SERVING

Calories: 230 | Total Fat: 4.5g | Cholesterol: 5mg | Sodium: 150mg | Total Carbs: 41g | Protein: 5g

Peanut Butter S' Mores

Prep Time: 10 minutes | Cook Time: 10 minutes | Serves 1

- 2 banana slices
- 1/2 teaspoon of natural peanut butter
- 1 marshmallow
- 2 chocolate wafers

1. Toast marshmallow over a fire.
2. On one chocolate wafer, spread the peanut butter.
3. Then top with the marshmallow, followed by the bananas and the second chocolate wafer.
4. Serve and enjoy!

PER SERVING

Calories: 109 | Protein: 1.7g | Carbs: 18.8g | Dietary Fiber: 0.5g | Sugar: 9.6g | Fat: 3.2g | Calcium: 0.9mg | Sodium: 86.7mg | Added Sugar: 3 g

Bacon and Tomato Frittata

Prep Time: 20 minutes | Cook Time: 20 minutes | Serves 4

- 1 carton (16 oz) fat-free egg product
- ¼ teaspoon salt-free garlic-and-herb seasoning
- 2 teaspoons canola oil
- 4 medium green onions, sliced (¼ cup)
- ½ cup sliced celery
- 2 large plum (Roma) tomatoes, sliced
- ¼ cup shredded sharp reduced-fat Cheddar cheese (2 oz)
- 2 tablespoons real bacon pieces (from 2.8-oz package)
- 2 tablespoons light sour cream, if desired

1. In medium bowl, mix egg product and garlic-and-herb seasoning | set aside.
2. In 10-inch nonstick ovenproof skillet, heat oil over medium heat. Add onions and celery | cook and stir 1 minute. Reduce heat to medium-low. Pour in egg mixture. Cook 6 to 9 minutes, gently lifting edges of cooked portions with spatula so that uncooked egg mixture can flow to bottom of skillet, until set.
3. Set oven control to broil. Top frittata with tomatoes, cheese and bacon. Broil with top 4 inches from heat 1 to 2 minutes or until cheese is melted. Top each serving with sour cream

PER SERVING

Calories: 110 | Total Fat: 4g | Cholesterol: 5mg | Sodium: 400mg | Total Carbs: 4g | Protein: 15g

Tropical Fruit 'n Ginger Oatmeal

Prep Time: 15 minutes | Cook Time: 45 minutes | Serves 4

- 2¼ cups water
- ¾ cup steel-cut oats
- 2 teaspoons finely chopped gingerroot
- ⅛ teaspoon salt
- ½ medium banana, mashed
- 1 container (6 oz) vanilla low-fat yogurt
- 1 medium mango, pitted, peeled and chopped (1 cup)
- ½ cup sliced fresh strawberries
- 2 tablespoons shredded coconut, toasted*
- 2 tablespoons chopped walnuts

1. In 1½-quart saucepan, heat water to boiling. Stir in oats, gingerroot and salt. Reduce heat | simmer gently uncovered 25 to 30 minutes, without stirring, until oats are tender yet slightly chewy | stir in banana. Divide oatmeal evenly among 4 bowls.
2. Top each serving with yogurt, mango, strawberries, coconut and walnuts. Serve immediately.

PER SERVING

Calories: 200 | Total Fat: 6g | Cholesterol: 0mg | Sodium: 110mg | Total Carbs: 31g | Protein: 5g

Tomato Parmesan Mini Quiches

Prep Time: 25 minutes | Cook Time: 25 minutes | Serves 6

- 1/2 cup of thinly sliced green onions
- 1 tablespoon of snipped fresh basil or 1 teaspoon of dried basil, crushed
- 1/4 teaspoon of black pepper
- Nonstick cooking spray
- 12 4-inch round thin slices of lower Sodium: cooked ham
- 1-1/4 cups of seeded and chopped Roma tomatoes
- 2/3 cup of finely shredded Parmesan cheese
- 6 eggs, lightly beaten

1. Preheat oven to 350 degrees f.
2. Use cooking spray to coat twelve 2 1/2-inch muffins.
3. Line prepared muffin cups with ham, and divide the tomatoes, basil, green onions, and pepper among cups.
4. Top with cheese and pour eggs over tomato mixture.
5. Bake until puffed and knife comes out clean, for about 20 to 25 minutes.
6. Cool in cups for about 5 minutes.
7. Remove from cups.
8. Top with additional green onions or fresh basil if you feel like it. Serve warm.

PER SERVING

Calories: 159 | Protein: 15g | Carbs: 5g | Dietary Fiber: 1g | Sugar: 3g | Fat: 8g | Sodium: 450mg.

Banana Pancakes

Prep Time: 15 minutes | **Cook Time:** 15 minutes | **Serves 2**

- 1 medium banana
- 2 large eggs

1. Puree banana and eggs in a blender until smooth.
2. Oil a large skillet lightly and heat over medium heat.
3. Use two tablespoons of batter for each of the pancakes.
4. Drop about four mounts of batter into the pan.
5. Cook for about 2 to 4 minutes until bubbles appear on the surface and the edges start to look dry.
6. Gently flip the pancakes using a thin spatula.
7. Cook for about 1 to 2 minutes more until browned on the bottom.
8. Transfer the pancakes to a plate.
9. Oil the pan lightly again and repeat with the rest of the batter.

PER SERVING

Calories: 124 | Protein: 6.9g | Carbs: 13.8g | Dietary Fiber: 1.5g | Sugar: 7.4g | Fat: 4.9g | Calcium: 31mg

Holiday Strata

Prep Time: 25 minutes | **Cook Time:** 1 hour | **Serves 8**

- 8 eggs
- 6 slices bacon, diced
- 4 breakfast sausages, casings removed and meat crumbled
- 1 onion, diced fine
- 1 pint cherry tomatoes
- 4 cup spinach
- 3 cup skim milk
- 1 cup reduced fat cheddar cheese, grated
- What you'll need from store cupboard:
- ½ loaf Italian bread, cut in 2-inch cubes
- 2 tsp Dijon mustard
- 1 tsp salt
- ¼ tsp pepper
- Butter flavored cooking spray

1. Spray a 13x9-inch baking dish with cooking spray.
2. Heat a large non-stick skillet over medium heat. Add bacon and sausage and cook until bacon is crisp, and sausage is cooked through, about 5-7 minutes. Transfer to paper towel lined plate. Drain all but 1 tablespoon of fat from the pan.
3. Add onion and cook until soft and golden brown, about 6 minutes.
4. Add tomatoes and spinach and cook until tomatoes start to soften and spinach wilts, about 2 minutes. Remove from heat and set aside to cool.
5. In a large bowl, beat eggs with milk, Dijon, salt and pepper. Mix in cheese, bread, bacon, sausage, and spinach mixture. Pour into prepared pan and cover with plastic wrap.
6. Refrigerate for two hours or overnight.
7. Heat oven to 359 degrees. Uncover and bake 1 hour, or until set in the center. Cool slightly before serving.

PER SERVING

Calories: 343 | Total Carbs: 24g | Net Carbs: 22g | Protein: 25g | Fat 16g | Sugar: 7g | Fiber: 2g

Kiwi Salsa with Chips
Prep Time: 5 minutes | Cook Time: 5 minutes | Serves 1

- 8 corn tortilla chips
- 2 tablespoons of chopped kiwi
- 2 tablespoons of tomatillo salsa

1. Stir kiwi into salsa.
2. Serve with chips.

PER SERVING

Calories: 158 | Protein: 2.3g | Carbs: 24.5g | Dietary Fiber: 2.2g | Sugar: 3.2g | Fat: 6g

Ham & Jicama Hash
Prep Time: 10 minutes | Cook Time: 15 minutes | Serves 4

- 6 eggs, beaten
- 2 cups jicama, grated
- 1 cup low fat cheddar cheese, grated
- 1 cup ham, diced
- Salt and pepper, to taste
- Nonstick cooking spray

1. Spray a large nonstick skillet with cooking spray and place over medium-high heat. Add jicama and cook, stirring occasionally, until it starts to brown, about 5 minutes.
2. Add remaining Ingredients and reduce heat to medium. Cook about 3 minutes, then flip over and cook until eggs are set, about 3-5 minutes more. Season with salt and pepper and serve.

PER SERVING

Calories: 221 | Total Carbs: 8g | Net Carbs: 5g | Protein: 21g | Fat 11g | Sugar: 2g | Fiber 3g

Grain Flapjacks

Prep Time: 15 minutes | Cook Time: 15 minutes | Serves 16

- 1/4 cup of refrigerated or frozen egg product, thawed, or 1 egg
- 1-3/4 cups of fat-free milk
- 1/4 cup of plain low-fat yogurt
- 3 tablespoons of cooking oil
- 1/2 cup of dried blueberries or currants
- 1-1/2 cups of all-purpose flour
- 1/2 cup of yellow cornmeal
- 2-1/2 teaspoons of baking powder
- 1/2 teaspoon of salt, 1/2 cup of regular rolled oats
- 3 tablespoons of packed brown sugar
- 1 (8 ounces) can of Pineapple chunks, drained and roughly chopped

1. Stir together the flour, baking powder, cornmeal, and salt in an extensive powder.
2. Combine brown sugar and oats in a blender or food processor.
3. Cover and blender until the oats are coarsely ground.
4. Stir the oat mixture into the flour and mix. In the center of the flour mixture, make a well. Combine egg, yogurt, milk, and oil in a medium bowl.
5. Beat using a fork until well combined.
6. Add the egg mixture all at once into the flour mixture.
7. Stir until well combined and let stand for about 10 minutes to thicken slightly, stirring once or twice. Gently fold in blueberries or currants if desired.
8. Coat an unheated nonstick griddle lightly using cooking spray.
9. Preheat over medium heat, and for each pancake, pour 1/4 cup of the batter into the hot griddle or maybe skillet.
10. Cook over medium heat until the pancakes are golden brown, turning to second sides when the pancakes have bubbly surfaces and edges, are dry for about 1 1/2 to 2 minutes on each side. Serve warm and top with pineapple chunks if you feel like it. Enjoy!

PER SERVING

Calories: 220 | Protein: 6.5g | Carbs: 34.9g | Dietary Fiber: 1.7g | Sugar: 8.5g | Fat: 6g

Roasted Veggies with Baked Eggs

Prep Time: 25 minutes | Cook Time: 9 hours | Serves 6

- 1 small red onion, cut into thin slices
- 2 tablespoons of olive oil
- 6 eggs
- 2 ounces of Manchego cheese, shredded (1/2 cup)
- 3 cups of small broccoli florets (about 1 inch in size)
- 12 ounces of yellow potatoes, such as Yukon Gold, cut into 1/2- to 3/4-inch pieces (about 2 cups)
- 1 large sweet potato, cut into 1/2- to 3/4-inch pieces (about 1 cup)
- 1/2 teaspoon of cracked black pepper

1. Preheat oven to 425 degrees f.
2. Coat about a 2-quart baking dish with nonstick cooking spray.
3. Combine broccoli, sweet potato, yellow potatoes, olive oil, onion, and 1/4 teaspoon of salt in a large bowl, tossing to coat vegetables.
4. Spread the veggie mixture evenly in the prepared pan and roast for about 10 minutes.s
5. Stir veggies and roast until veggies are tender and starting to brown for about 5 minutes.
6. Remove from oven. Then spread the veggies evenly in the baking dish | cool.
7. Cover and chill for about 8 to 24 hours in the refrigerator.
8. Let chilled vegetables stand for about 30 minutes at room -temp.
9. Meanwhile, preheat the oven to 375 degrees f.
10. Bake vegetables for about 5 minutes, uncovered. Remove from the oven and mix about 6 wells in the layer of vegetables.
11. Break an egg into each well. Then bake for about 5 minutes more.
12. Sprinkle with cheese and bake until eggs whites are set and yolks start to thicken for about 5 to 10 minutes.
13. Sprinkle with pepper. Serve & enjoy!

PER SERVING

Calories: 232 | Protein: 11.1g | Carbs: 21.4g | Dietary Fiber: 3.5g | Sugar: 3.8g | Fat: 12g

Corn Cakes & Eggs

Prep Time: 45 minutes | Cook Time: 45 minutes | Serves 6

- 1-1/4 cups of buttermilk
- 8 large eggs, divided
- 2 tablespoons of canola oil
- 1/4 teaspoon of ground pepper, divided
- 1 cup of shredded reduced-fat Cheddar cheese (4 ounces), divided
- 4 green onions
- 2/3 cup of all-purpose flour
- 2/3 cup of yellow cornmeal
- 2 teaspoons of baking powder
- 1/8 teaspoon of salt
- 2-1/2 cups of chopped tomatoes
- 1 tablespoon of lemon juice
- 1/4 teaspoon of salt, divided

1. Stir cornmeal, flour, 1/8 teaspoon of salt, and baking powder in a medium bowl.
2. In a small bowl, beat about 2 eggs. Add oil, buttermilk, and stir to combine. In the center of the flour mixture, make a well and stir in the buttermilk mixture just until well moistened.
3. Fold in half cup cheese and transfer to a sealable plastic bag.
4. Thinly slice the green onions, separating the green and white parts.
5. Combine the tomatoes, onion whites, lemon juice, and 1/8 teaspoon of pepper in a medium bowl.
6. Coat a nonstick griddle with cooking spray lightly and heat over medium heat. Snip a 1/2 inch hold in the bottom of the batter bag.
7. Working in batches, pipe a six-inch ring of batter onto the hot griddle for each corncake.
8. Break an egg into each ring quickly and sprinkle with some salt and 1/8 teaspoon of pepper.
9. Cook for about 3 to 4 minutes until the corncakes are bubbly on top.
10. Turn them over and sprinkle with some of the cheese.
11. Cook, until the yolks are the desired doneness and corncakes are golden for about 1 to 2 minutes more.
12. Keep warm while cooking the rest of the corncakes.
13. And sprinkle with onion greens and serve with salsa.

PER SERVING

Calories: 325 | Protein: 18g | Carbs: 31g | Dietary Fiber: 2g | Sugar: 5g | Fat: 15g | Sodium: 629mg.

Triple-Berry Oatmeal Muesli

Prep Time: 25 minutes | Cook Time: 40 minutes | Serves 6

- 2¾ cups old-fashioned oats or rolled barley
- ½ cup sliced almonds
- 2 containers (6 oz each) banana crème or French vanilla fat-free yogurt
- 1½ cups milk
- ¼ cup ground flaxseed or flaxseed meal
- ½ cup fresh blueberries
- ½ cup fresh raspberries
- ½ cup sliced fresh strawberries

1. Heat oven to 350°F. On cookie sheet, spread oats and almonds. Bake 18 to 20 minutes, stirring occasionally, until light golden brown | cool 15 minutes.
2. In large bowl, mix yogurt and milk until well blended. Stir in oats, almonds and flaxseed. Divide muesli evenly among 6 bowls. Top each serving with berries.

PER SERVING

Calories: 320 | Total Fat: 10g | Cholesterol: 5mg | Sodium: 65mg | Total Carbs: 46g | Protein: 11g

Hawaiian Breakfast Bake

Prep Time: 10 minutes | Cook Time: 20 minutes | Serves 6

- 6 slice ham, sliced thin
- 6 eggs
- ¼ cup reduced fat cheddar cheese, grated
- 6 pineapple slices
- 2 tbsp. salsa
- ½ tsp seasoning blend, salt-free

1. Heat oven to 350 degrees.
2. Line 6 muffin cups, or ramekins with sliced ham. Layer with cheese, salsa, and pineapple.
3. Crack one egg into each cup, sprinkle with seasoning blend.
4. If using ramekins place them on a baking sheet, bake 20-25 minutes or until egg whites are completely set but yolks are still soft. Serve immediately.

PER SERVING

Calories: 135 | Total Carbs: 5g | Net Carbs: 4g | Protein: 12g | Fat 8g | Sugar: 3g | Fiber: 1g

Italian Breakfast Bake

Prep Time: 10 minutes | Cook Time: 1 hour | Serves 8

- 19 oz. pkg. mild Italian sausages, remove casings
- 1 yellow onion, diced
- 8 eggs
- 2 cup half-and-half
- 2 cup reduced fat cheddar cheese, grated
- ¼ cup fresh parsley, diced
- 2 tbsp. butter, divided
- 1/2 loaf bread, (chapter 14), cut in cubes
- 1 tsp salt
- ¼ tsp pepper
- ¼ tsp red pepper flakes
- Nonstick cooking spray

1. Spray a 9x13-inch baking dish with cooking spray.
2. Melt 1 tablespoon butter in a skillet over medium heat. Add sausage and cook, breaking up with a spatula, until no longer pink. Transfer to a large bowl.
3. Add remaining tablespoon butter to the skillet with the onion and cook until soft, 3-5 minutes. Add to sausage with the cheese and bread cubes.
4. In a separate bowl, whisk together eggs, half-n-half, and seasonings. Pour over sausage mixture, tossing to mix all Ingredients. Pour into prepared baking dish, cover and chill 2 hours, or overnight.
5. Heat oven to 350 degrees. Remove cover and bake 50-60 minutes, or a knife inserted in center comes out clean. Serve immediately garnished with parsley.

PER SERVING

Calories: 300 | Total Carbs: 6g | Net Carbs: 5g | Protein: 22g | Fat: 20g | Sugar: 4g | Fiber: 1g

Hot Maple Porridge

Prep Time: 2 minutes | Cook Time: 1 minutes | Serves 1

- 1 tsp margarine
- 1/2 cup water
- 2 tbsp. flax meal
- 1 tbsp. almond flour
- 1 tbsp. coconut flour
- 1 tsp Splenda
- ¼ tsp maple extract
- Pinch salt

1. In a microwave safe bowl, combine all Ingredients, except margarine, and mix thoroughly.
2. Microwave on high for one minute.
3. Stir in margarine and serve.

PER SERVING

Calories: 143 | Total Carbs: 9g | Net Carbs: 2g | Protein: 5g | Fat: 1g | Sugar: 0g | Fiber: 7g

Chapter 4
Soups, Salads, and Stews

Cucumber, Tomato, and Avocado Salad

Prep Time: 10 minutes | Cook Time: 0 minutes | Serves 4

- 1 cup cherry tomatoes, halved
- 1 large cucumber, chopped
- 1 small red onion, thinly sliced
- 1 avocado, diced
- 2 tablespoons chopped fresh dill
- 2 tablespoons extra-virgin olive oil
- Juice of 1 lemon
- ¼ teaspoon salt
- ¼ teaspoon freshly ground black pepper

1. In a large mixing bowl, combine the tomatoes, cucumber, onion, avocado, and dill.
2. In a small bowl, combine the oil, lemon juice, salt, and pepper, and mix well.
3. Drizzle the dressing over the vegetables and toss to combine. Serve.

PER SERVING

Calories: 151 | Total Fat: 12g | Protein: 2g | Carbs: 11g | Sugar: 4g | Fiber: 4g | Sodium: 128mg

Cabbage Slaw Salad

Prep Time: 15 minutes | Cook Time: 0 minutes | Serves 6

- 2 cups finely chopped green cabbage
- 2 cups finely chopped red cabbage
- 2 cups grated carrots
- 3 scallions, both white and green parts, sliced
- 2 tablespoons extra-virgin olive oil
- 2 tablespoons rice vinegar
- 1 teaspoon honey
- 1 garlic clove, minced
- ¼ teaspoon salt

1. In a large bowl, toss together the green and red cabbage, carrots, and scallions.
2. In a small bowl, whisk together the oil, vinegar, honey, garlic, and salt.
3. Pour the dressing over the veggies and mix to thoroughly combine.
4. Serve immediately, or cover and chill for several hours before serving.

PER SERVING

Calories: 80 | Total Fat: 5g | Protein: 1g | Carbs: 10g | Sugar: 6g | Fiber: 3g | Sodium: 126mg

Three Bean and Basil Salad

Prep Time: 10 minutes | **Cook Time:** 0 minutes | **Serves 8**

- 1 (15-ounce) can low-Sodium: chickpeas, drained and rinsed
- 1 (15-ounce) can low-Sodium: kidney beans, drained and rinsed
- 1 (15-ounce) can low-Sodium: white beans, drained and rinsed
- 1 red bell pepper, seeded and finely chopped
- ¼ cup chopped scallions, both white and green parts
- ¼ cup finely chopped fresh basil
- 3 garlic cloves, minced
- 2 tablespoons extra-virgin olive oil
- 1 tablespoon red wine vinegar
- 1 teaspoon Dijon mustard
- ¼ teaspoon freshly ground black pepper

1. In a large mixing bowl, combine the chickpeas, kidney beans, white beans, bell pepper, scallions, basil, and garlic. Toss gently to combine.
2. In a small bowl, combine the olive oil, vinegar, mustard, and pepper. Toss with the salad.
3. Cover and refrigerate for an hour before serving, to allow the flavors to mix.

PER SERVING

Calories: 193 | Total Fat: 5g | Protein: 10g | Carbs: 29g | Sugar: 3g | Fiber: 8g | Sodium: 246mg

Warm Barley and Squash Salad with Balsamic Vinaigrette

Prep Time: 20 minutes | **Cook Time:** 40 minutes | **Serves 8**

- 1 small butternut squash
- 3 teaspoons plus 2 tablespoons extra-virgin olive oil, divided
- 2 cups broccoli florets
- 1 cup pearl barley
- 1 cup toasted chopped walnuts
- 2 cups baby kale
- ½ red onion, sliced
- 2 tablespoons balsamic vinegar
- 2 garlic cloves, minced
- ½ teaspoon salt
- ¼ teaspoon freshly ground black pepper

1. Preheat the oven to 400°F. Line a baking sheet with parchment paper.
2. 2.Peel and seed the squash, and cut it into dice. In a large bowl, toss the squash with 2 teaspoons of olive oil. Transfer to the prepared baking sheet and roast for 20 minutes.
3. While the squash is roasting, toss the broccoli in the same bowl with 1 teaspoon of olive oil. After 20 minutes, flip the squash and push it to one side of the baking sheet. Add the broccoli to the other side and continue to roast for 20 more minutes until tender.
4. While the veggies are roasting, in a medium pot, cover the barley with several inches of water. Bring to a boil, then reduce the heat, cover, and simmer for 30 minutes until tender. Drain and rinse.
5. Transfer the barley to a large bowl, and toss with the cooked squash and broccoli, walnuts, kale, and onion.
6. In a small bowl, mix the remaining 2 tablespoons of olive oil, balsamic vinegar, garlic, salt, and pepper. Toss the salad with the dressing and serve.

PER SERVING

Calories: 274 | Total Fat: 15g | Protein: 6g | Carbs: 32g | Sugar: 3g | Fiber: 7g | Sodium: 144mg

Chilled Parsley-Gazpacho

Prep Time: 10 minutes | Cook Time: 2 hours | Serves 1

- 4-5 middle sized tomatoes
- 2 tablespoon olive oil, and cold pressed
- 2 large cups parsley
- 2 ripe avocados
- 2 garlic cloves, diced
- 2 limes, juiced
- 4 cups vegetable broth
- 1 middle sized cucumber
- 2 small red onions, diced
- 1 teaspoon dried oregano
- 1½ teaspoon paprika powder
- salt and black pepper, to taste
- ½ teaspoon cayenne pepper

1. In a suitable pan, heat up olive oil and sauté onions and garlic until translucent.
2. Blend avocado, tomatoes, lime juice, parsley, vegetable broth, cucumber, and onion-garlic mix until smooth. Add some water if desired, and season with cayenne pepper, paprika powder, oregano, salt and pepper.
3. Blend again and put in the fridge for at least 1-½ hours. You can add chives or dill to the gazpacho. Enjoy!

PER SERVING

Calories: 48 | Total Carbs: 12 g | Fat: 0.8g | Net Carbs: 2g | Protein: 1g | Sugar: 1g | Fiber: 2g

Beef and Vegetable Soup

Prep Time: 10 minutes | Cook Time: 15 minutes | Serves 4

- 1 pound (454g) ground beef
- 1 onion, chopped
- 2 celery stalks, chopped
- 1 carrot, chopped
- 1 teaspoon dried rosemary
- 6 cups low-Sodium: beef or chicken broth
- ½ teaspoon sea salt
- ⅛ teaspoon freshly ground black pepper
- 2 cups peas

1. In a large pot over medium-high heat, cook the ground beef, crumbling with the side of a spoon, until browned, about 5 minutes.
2. Add the onion, celery, carrot, and rosemary. Cook, stirring occasionally, until the vegetables start to soften, about 5 minutes.
3. Add the broth, salt, pepper, and peas. Bring to a simmer. Reduce the heat and simmer, stirring, until warmed through, about 5 minutes more.

PER SERVING

Calories: 356 | Fat: 17.1g | Protein: 34.1g | Carbs: 17.9g | Fiber: 5.1g | Sugar: 12.6g | Sodium: 363mg

Pumpkin White Bean Soup

Prep Time: 10 minutes | Cook Time: 40 minutes | Serves 4

- 1 ½ pound pumpkin
- ½ pound yams
- ½ pound white beans
- 1 onion
- 2 cloves of garlic
- 1 tablespoon of olive oil
- 1 tablespoon of spices
- 1 tablespoon of sage
- 1 ½ quart water
- A spot of salt and pepper

1. Cut the pumpkin in shapes, cut the onion and cut the garlic, the spices and the sage into fine pieces.
2. Sauté the onion and also the garlic in olive oil for around 2 or 3 minutes. Add the pumpkin, spices and sage and fry for an additional 5 minutes.
3. At that point, add the water and cook for around 30 minutes until vegetables are delicate. At long last add the beans and some salt and pepper. Cook for an additional 5 minutes and serve right away. Serve.

PER SERVING

Calories: 78 | Total Carbs: 12g | Net Carbs: 2g | Protein: 1g | Fat: 12g | Sugar: 1g | Fiber: 2g

Carrot Mushrooms Soup

Prep Time: 10 minutes | Cook Time: 20 minutes | Serves 1-2

- 4 carrots
- 4 potatoes
- 10 large mushrooms
- ½ white onion
- 2 tablespoon olive oil
- 3 cups vegetable stock
- 2 tablespoon parsley
- Salt and white pepper, to taste

1. Wash and strip carrots and potatoes and dice them. Heat the vegetable stock in a pot over medium heat.
2. Cook carrots and potatoes for around 15 minutes. Meanwhile, shape onion and braise them in a container with olive oil for around 3 minutes. Wash mushrooms, slice them to the wanted size and add to the container, cooking approx. An additional 5 minutes, blending at times. Blend carrots, vegetable stock and potatoes, and put the substance of the skillet into the pot.
3. When nearly done, season with parsley, salt and pepper and serve hot.

PER SERVING

Calories: 75 | Total Carbs: 13g | Fat: 1.8g | Net Carbs: 0.5g | Protein: 1 g | Sugar: 1g | Fiber: 2g

Rainbow Black Bean Salad

Prep Time: 15 minutes | Cook Time: 0 minutes | Serves 5

- 1 (15-ounce) can low-Sodium: black beans, drained and rinsed
- 1 avocado, diced
- 1 cup cherry
- tomatoes, halved
- 1 cup chopped baby spinach
- ½ cup finely chopped red bell pepper
- ¼ cup finely chopped jicama
- ½ cup chopped scallions, both white and green parts
- ¼ cup chopped fresh cilantro
- 2 tablespoons freshly squeezed lime juice
- 1 tablespoon extra-virgin olive oil
- 2 garlic cloves, minced
- 1 teaspoon honey
- ¼ teaspoon salt
- ¼ teaspoon freshly ground black pepper

1. In a large bowl, combine the black beans, avocado, tomatoes, spinach, bell pepper, jicama, scallions, and cilantro.
2. In a small bowl, mix the lime juice, oil, garlic, honey, salt, and pepper. Add to the salad and toss.
3. Chill for 1 hour before serving.

PER SERVING

Calories: 169 | Total Fat: 7g | Protein: 6g | Carbs: 22g | Sugar: 3g | Fiber: 9g | Sodium: 235mg

Avocado-Broccoli Soup

Prep Time: 10 minutes | Cook Time: 15 minutes | Serves 1-2

- 2-3 flowers broccoli
- 1 avocado
- 1 yellow onion
- 1 green or red pepper
- 1 celery stalk
- 2 cups vegetable broth
- Celtic sea salt to taste

1. Heat vegetable stock in a pot. Add hacked onion and broccoli, and warm for a few minutes.
2. At that point, put in a blender, add the avocado, pepper and celery and blend until the soup is smooth. Serve warm.

PER SERVING

Calories: 60g | Total Carbs: 11g | Fat: 2 g | Net Carbs: 2g | Protein: 2g | Sugar: 1g | Fiber: 2g

Carrot Millet Soup

Prep Time: 7 minutes | Cook Time: 40 minutes | Serves 3

- 2 cups cauliflower pieces
- 1 cup potatoes, cubed
- 2 cups vegetables stock
- 3 tablespoons low-fat Swiss Emmenthal cheddar, cubed
- 2 tablespoons chives
- 1 tablespoon pumpkin seeds
- 1 touch of nutmeg and cayenne pepper
- salt

1. Cook cauliflower and potato in vegetable stock until delicate and blend with a blender. Season the soup with nutmeg and cayenne, and possibly somewhat salt and pepper.
2. Add Emmenthal cheddar and chives and mix a couple of moments until the soup is smooth and prepared to serve. Enhance with pumpkin seeds.

PER SERVING

Calories: 65 | Total Carbs: 15g | Fat: 1g | Net Carbs: 0.5g | Protein: 2g | Sugar: 1g | Fiber: 2g

Down South Corn Soup

Prep Time: 10 minutes | Cook Time: 35 minutes | Serves 8

- 1 tablespoon extra-virgin olive oil
- ½ Vidalia onion, minced
- 2 garlic cloves, minced
- 3 cups chopped cabbage
- 1 small cauliflower, broken into florets or 1 (10-ounce) bag frozen cauliflower
- 1 (10-ounce) bag frozen corn
- 1 cup Vegetable Broth or store-bought low-Sodium: vegetable broth
- 1 teaspoon smoked paprika
- 1 teaspoon ground cumin
- 1 teaspoon dried dill
- ½ teaspoon freshly ground black pepper
- 1 cup plain unsweetened cashew milk

1. In a large stockpot, heat the oil over medium heat.
2. Add the onion and garlic, and sauté, stirring to prevent the garlic from scorching, for 3 to 5 minutes, or until translucent.
3. Add the cabbage and a splash of water, cover, and cook for 5 minutes, or until tender.
4. Add the cauliflower, corn, broth, paprika, cumin, dill, and pepper. Cover and cook for 20 minutes, or until tender.
5. Add the cashew milk and stir well. Cover and cook for 5 minutes, letting the flavors come together.

PER SERVING

Calories: 120 | Total Fat: 4g | Cholesterol: 0mg | Sodium: 53mg | Total Carbs: 18g | Sugar: 4g | Fiber: 3g | Protein: 3g

Green Salad with Blackberries, Goat Cheese, and Sweet Potatoes

Prep Time: 15 minutes | **Cook Time:** 20 minutes | **Serves 4**

- 1 pint blackberries
- 2 tablespoons red wine vinegar
- 1 tablespoon honey
- 3 tablespoons extra-virgin olive oil
- ¼ teaspoon salt
- Freshly ground black pepper
- 1 sweet potato, cubed
- 1 teaspoon extra-virgin olive oil
- 8 cups salad greens (baby spinach, spicy greens, romaine)
- ½ red onion, sliced
- ¼ cup crumbled goat cheese

1. In a blender jar, combine the blackberries, vinegar, honey, oil, salt, and pepper, and process until smooth. Set aside.
2. Preheat the oven to 425°F. Line a baking sheet with parchment paper.
3. In a medium mixing bowl, toss the sweet potato with the olive oil. Transfer to the prepared baking sheet and roast for 20 minutes, stirring once halfway through, until tender. Remove and cool for a few minutes.
4. In a large bowl, toss the greens with the red onion and cooled sweet potato, and drizzle with the vinaigrette. Serve topped with 1 tablespoon of goat cheese per serving.

PER SERVING

Calories: 196 | Total Fat: 12g | Protein: 3g | Carbs: 21g | Sugar: 10g | Fiber: 6g | Sodium: 184mg

Herbed Chicken Meatball Wraps

Prep Time: 10 minutes | **Cook Time:** 20 minutes | **Serves 6**

- 1 pound ground chicken
- 3 scallions, both white and green parts, finely chopped
- 2 garlic cloves, minced
- 2 tablespoons chopped fresh mint
- ½ teaspoon dried oregano
- 1 egg, lightly beaten
- 12 large lettuce leaves
- 1 medium red bell pepper, seeded and cut into strips
- 1 carrot, cut into strips
- 1 recipe Cucumber-Yogurt Dip

1. Preheat the oven to 400°F. Line a baking sheet with parchment paper.
2. In a large mixing bowl, combine the chicken, scallions, garlic, mint, oregano, and egg. Stir well.
3. Using your hands, form the meat mixture into balls about the size of a tablespoon, making about 24 balls. Arrange on the prepared baking sheet.
4. Bake for 10 minutes, flip with a spatula, and continue baking for an additional 10 minutes until the meatballs are cooked through.
5. In each lettuce leaf, place two meatballs and several bell pepper and carrot strips. Top with 2 tablespoons of Cucumber-Yogurt Dip. Wrap the leaves around the filling and serve with the dip.

PER SERVING

Calories: 220 | Total Fat: 12g | Protein: 23g | Carbs: 6g | Sugar: 3g | Fiber: 2g | Sodium: 199mg

Pumpkin Tomato Soup

Prep Time: 15 minutes | **Cook Time:** 30 minutes | **Serves 4**

- 4 cups of water
- 14 ounces tomatoes, stripped and diced
- 1 sweet pumpkin
- 5 yellow onions
- 1 tablespoon olive oil
- 2 teaspoons salt
- 1 pinch of cayenne pepper
- Bunch of parsley, chopped

1. Sauté chopped onion with some oil in a suitable pot. Cut the pumpkin down the middle | at that point, remove the stem and scoop out the seeds.
2. At long last, scoop out the fragile living creature and put it in the pot. Add the tomatoes and the water likewise and cook for around 20 minutes. At that point, empty the soup into a food processor and blend well for a couple of moments. Sprinkle with salt, pepper and other spices. Fill bowls and top with parsley. Serve!

PER SERVING

Calories: 78 | Total Carbs: 20g | Net Carbs: 2g | Protein: 1.5g | Fat: 0.5g | Sugar: 1g | Fiber: 2g

Fast Split Pea Soup

Prep Time: 8 minutes | **Cook Time:** 15 minutes | **Serves 4**

- 1½ cups dried green split peas, rinsed and drained
- 4 cups vegetable broth or water
- 2 celery stalks, chopped
- 1 medium onion, chopped
- 2 carrots, chopped
- 3 garlic cloves, minced
- 1 teaspoon herbes de Provence
- 1 teaspoon liquid smoke
- Kosher salt and freshly ground black pepper, to taste
- Shredded carrot, for garnish (optional)

1. In the electric pressure cooker, combine the peas, broth, celery, onion, carrots, garlic, herbes de Provence, and liquid smoke.
2. Close and lock the lid of the pressure cooker. Set the valve to sealing.
3. Cook on high pressure for 15 minutes.
4. When the cooking is complete, hit Cancel and allow the pressure to release naturally for 10 minutes, then quick release any remaining pressure.
5. Once the pin drops, unlock and remove the lid.
6. Stir the soup and season with salt and pepper.
7. Spoon into serving bowls and sprinkle shredded carrots on top (if using).

PER SERVING

Calories: 285 | Fat: 1.1g | Protein: 19.1g | Carbs: 51.9g | Fiber: 21.1g | Sugar: 9.0g | Sodium: 61mg

Clam Chowder

Prep Time: 10 minutes | Cook Time: 15 minutes | Serves 4

- 2 tablespoons extra-virgin olive oil
- 3 slices pepper bacon, chopped
- 1 onion, chopped
- 1 red bell pepper, seeded and chopped
- 1 fennel bulb, chopped
- 3 tablespoons flour
- 5 cups low-Sodium: or unsalted chicken broth
- 6 ounces (170g) chopped canned clams, undrained
- ½ teaspoon sea salt
- ½ cup milk

1. In a large pot over medium-high heat, heat the olive oil until it shimmers. Add the bacon and cook, stirring, until browned, about 4 minutes. Remove the bacon from the fat with a slotted spoon, and set it aside on a plate.
2. Add the onion, bell pepper, and fennel to the fat in the pot. Cook, stirring occasionally, until the vegetables are soft, about 5 minutes. Add the flour and cook, stirring constantly, for 1 minute. Add the broth, clams, and salt. Bring to a simmer. Cook, stirring, until the soup thickens, about 5 minutes more.
3. Stir in the milk and return the bacon to the pot. Cook, stirring, 1 minute more.

PER SERVING

Calories: 336 | Fat: 20.1g | Protein: 20.1g | Carbs: 20.9g | Fiber: 3.1g | Sugar: 11.4g | Sodium: 495mg

Chicken and Egg Noodle Soup

Prep Time: 15 minutes | Cook Time: 30 minutes | Serves 12

- 2 tablespoons avocado oil
- 1 medium onion, chopped
- 3 celery stalks, chopped
- 1 teaspoon kosher salt
- ¼ teaspoon freshly ground black pepper
- 2 teaspoons minced garlic
- 5 large carrots, peeled and cut into ¼-inch-thick rounds
- 3 pounds (1.4 kg) bone-in chicken breasts (about 3)
- 4 cups low-Sodium: chicken broth
- 4 cups water
- 2 tablespoons soy sauce
- 6 ounces (170 g) whole grain wide egg noodles

1. Set the electric pressure cooker to the Sauté setting. When the pot is hot, pour in the avocado oil.
2. Sauté the onion, celery, salt, and pepper for 3 to 5 minutes or until the vegetables begin to soften.
3. Add the garlic and carrots, and stir to mix well. Hit Cancel.
4. Add the chicken to the pot, meat-side down. Add the broth, water, and soy sauce. Close and lock the lid of the pressure cooker. Set the valve to sealing.
5. Cook on high pressure for 20 minutes.
6. When the cooking is complete, hit Cancel and quick release the pressure. Unlock and remove the lid.
7. Using tongs, remove the chicken breasts to a cutting board. Hit Sauté/More and bring the soup to a boil.
8. Add the noodles and cook for 4 to 5 minutes or until the noodles are al dente.
9. While the noodles are cooking, use two forks to shred the chicken. Add the meat back to the pot and save the bones to make more bone broth.
10. Season with additional pepper, if desired, and serve.

PER SERVING

Calories: 331 | Fat: 15.1g | Protein: 32.1g | Carbs: 16.9g | Fiber: 4.1g | Sugar: 3.0g | Sodium: 450mg

Eggplant Stew

Prep Time: 20 minutes | Cook Time: 8 minutes | Serves 4

- 2 tablespoons avocado oil
- 1 large onion, minced
- 2 garlic cloves, minced
- 1 teaspoon ras el hanout spice blend or curry powder
- ¼ teaspoon cayenne pepper
- 1 teaspoon kosher salt
- 1 cup vegetable broth or water
- 1 tablespoon tomato paste
- 2 cups chopped eggplant
- 2 medium gold potatoes, peeled and chopped
- 4 ounces (113 g) tomatillos, husks removed, chopped
- 1 (14-ounce / 397-g) can diced tomatoes

1. Set the electric pressure cooker to the Sauté setting. When the pot is hot, pour in the avocado oil.
2. Sauté the onion for 3 to 5 minutes, until it begins to soften. Add the garlic, ras el hanout, cayenne, and salt. Cook and stir for about 30 seconds. Hit Cancel.
3. Stir in the broth and tomato paste. Add the eggplant, potatoes, tomatillos, and tomatoes with their juices.
4. Close and lock the lid of the pressure cooker. Set the valve to sealing.
5. Cook on high pressure for 3 minutes.
6. When the cooking is complete, hit Cancel and allow the pressure to release naturally.
7. Once the pin drops, unlock and remove the lid.
8. Stir well and spoon into serving bowls.

PER SERVING

Calories: 215 | Fat: 8.1g | Protein: 4.1g | Carbs: 27.9g | Fiber: 8.1g | Sugar: 9.0g | Sodium: 736mg

Tuna, Hummus, and Veggie Wraps

Prep Time: 10 minutes | Cook Time: 0 minutes | Serves 2

- 1 cup from 1 (15-ounce) can low-Sodium: chickpeas, drained and rinsed
- 2 tablespoons tahini
- 1 tablespoon extra-virgin olive oil
- 1 garlic clove
- Juice of ½ lemon
- ¼ teaspoon salt
- 2 tablespoons water
- 4 large lettuce leaves
- 1 (5-ounce) can chunk light tuna packed in water, drained
- 1 red bell pepper, seeded and cut into strips
- 1 cucumber, sliced

1. In a blender jar, combine the chickpeas, tahini, olive oil, garlic, lemon juice, salt, and water. Process until smooth. Taste and adjust with additional lemon juice or salt, as needed.
2. On each lettuce leaf, spread 1 tablespoon of hummus, and divide the tuna among the leaves. Top each with several strips of red pepper and cucumber slices.
3. Roll up the lettuce leaves, folding in the two shorter sides and rolling away from you, like a burrito. Serve.

PER SERVING

Calories: 191 | Total Fat: 5g | Protein: 26g | Carbs: 15g | Sugar: 6g | Fiber: 4g | Sodium: 357mg

Thai-Style Chicken Roll-Ups

Prep Time: 15 minutes | Cook Time: 0 minutes | Serves 4

- 1½ cups shredded cooked chicken breast
- 1 cup bean sprouts
- 1 cup shredded green cabbage
- ½ cup shredded carrots
- ¼ cup chopped scallions, both white and green parts
- ¼ cup chopped fresh cilantro
- 2 tablespoons natural peanut butter
- 2 tablespoons water
- 1 tablespoon rice wine vinegar
- 1 garlic clove, minced
- ¼ teaspoon salt
- 4 (8-inch) low-carb whole-wheat tortillas

1. In a large mixing bowl, toss the chicken breast, bean sprouts, cabbage, carrots, scallions, and cilantro.
2. In a medium bowl, whisk together the peanut butter, water, rice vinegar, garlic, and salt.
3. Fill each tortilla with about 1 cup of the chicken and vegetable mixture, and spoon a tablespoon of sauce over the filling.
4. Fold in two opposite sides of the tortilla and roll up. Serve.

PER SERVING

Calories: 210 | Total Fat: 8g | Protein: 21g | Carbs: 17g | Sugar: 3g | Fiber: 10g | Sodium: 360mg

Chapter 5
Chicken and Poultry

Skillet-Blackened Chicken

Prep Time: 20 minutes | Cook Time: 20 minutes | Serves 4

- 2 medium boneless, skinless chicken breasts
- ½ teaspoon paprika
- Juice of 1 lemon
- ½ cup water
- 2 teaspoons Blackened Rub
- 1 tablespoon canola oil or sunflower oil

1. In a small bowl, massage the chicken all over with the paprika. Mix with the lemon juice and water. Set aside to marinate for 15 minutes.
2. Remove the chicken from the marinade, and shake off the excess liquid.
3. Coat the chicken all over with the rub.
4. Heat a large cast iron pan over medium heat. Pour in the oil. Add the chicken and cook for 5 to 7 minutes on each side, or until cooked through.
5. Remove the chicken from the heat, and let rest for 5 minutes.
6. Divide each breast into two portions. Serve hot, with Stewed Green Beans.

PER SERVING

Calories: 95 | Total Fat: 4g | Cholesterol: 33mg | Sodium: 40mg | Total Carbs: 0g | Sugar: 0g | Fiber: 0g | Protein: 13g

Buttermilk-Ginger Smothered Chicken

Prep Time: 30 minutes | Cook Time: 20 minutes | Serves 8

- 8 boneless, skinless chicken thighs
- 2 cups low-fat buttermilk
- ½ bunch fresh chives, thinly sliced
- ½ bunch fresh cilantro, thinly sliced
- 2 garlic cloves, minced
- 1 teaspoon ground ginger

1. Preheat the oven to 375°F.
2. In a large bowl, combine the chicken, buttermilk, chives, cilantro, garlic, and ginger, coating the chicken thoroughly. Cover and put in the refrigerator to marinate for at least 30 minutes.
3. Place the chicken in a Dutch oven and cover. Transfer to the oven and cook for 20 minutes, or until the chicken is moist on the inside and caramelized on the outside.
4. Serve with Grilled Hearts of Romaine with Buttermilk Dressing

PER SERVING

Calories: 157 | Total Fat: 5g | Cholesterol: 97mg | Sodium: 165mg | Total Carbs: 3g | Sugar: 3g | Fiber: 0g | Protein: 24g

Creamy Garlic Chicken with Broccoli

Prep Time: 5 minutes | Cook Time: 15 minutes | Serves 4

- ½ cup uncooked brown rice or quinoa
- 4 (4-ounce) boneless, skinless chicken breasts
- ¼ teaspoon salt
- ¼ teaspoon freshly ground black pepper
- 1 teaspoon garlic powder, divided
- Avocado oil cooking spray
- 3 cups fresh or frozen broccoli florets
- 1 cup half-and-half

1. Cook the rice according to the package instructions.
2. Meanwhile, season both sides of the chicken breasts with the salt, pepper, and ½ teaspoon of garlic powder.
3. Heat a large skillet over medium-low heat. When hot, coat the cooking surface with cooking spray and add the chicken and broccoli in a single layer.
4. Cook for 4 minutes, then flip the chicken breasts over and cover. Cook for 5 minutes more.
5. Add the half-and-half and remaining ½ teaspoon of garlic powder to the skillet and stir. Increase the heat to high and simmer for 2 minutes.
6. Divide the rice into four equal portions. Top each portion with 1 chicken breast and one-quarter of the broccoli and cream sauce.

PER SERVING

Calories: 303 | Total Fat: 10g | Protein: 33g | Carbs: 22g | Sugar: 4g | Fiber: 3g | Sodium: 271mg

Greek Chicken Stuffed Peppers

Prep Time: 5 minutes | Cook Time: 30 minutes | Serves 4

- 2 large red bell peppers
- 2 teaspoons extra-virgin olive oil, divided
- ½ cup uncooked brown rice or quinoa
- 4 (4-ounce) boneless, skinless chicken breasts
- ¼ teaspoon garlic powder
- ¼ teaspoon onion powder
- ⅛ teaspoon dried thyme
- ½ teaspoon dried oregano
- ½ cup crumbled feta

1. Cut the bell peppers in half and remove the seeds.
2. In a large skillet, heat 1 teaspoon of olive oil over low heat. When hot, place the bell pepper halves cut-side up in the skillet. Cover and cook for 20 minutes.
3. Cook the rice according to the package instructions.
4. Meanwhile, cut the chicken into 1-inch pieces.
5. In a medium skillet, heat the remaining 1 teaspoon of olive oil over medium-low heat. When hot, add the chicken.
6. Season the chicken with the garlic powder, onion powder, thyme, and oregano.
7. Cook for 5 minutes, stirring occasionally, until cooked through.
8. In a large bowl, combine the cooked rice and chicken. Scoop one-quarter of the chicken and rice mixture into each pepper half, cover, and cook for 10 minutes over low heat.
9. Top each pepper half with 2 tablespoons of crumbled feta.

PER SERVING

Calories: 288 | Total Fat: 10g | Protein: 32g | Carbs: 20g | Sugar: 4g | Fiber: 4g | Sodium: 267mg

Teriyaki Chicken and Broccoli

Prep Time: 5 minutes | Cook Time: 20 minutes | Serves 4

- ½ cup water
- 2 tablespoons low-Sodium: soy sauce
- 2 tablespoons honey
- 1 tablespoon rice vinegar
- ¼ teaspoon garlic powder
- Pinch ground ginger
- 1 tablespoon cornstarch
- 1 tablespoon sesame oil
- 4 (4-ounce) boneless, skinless chicken breasts, cut into bite-size cubes
- 1 (12-ounce) bag frozen broccoli
- 1 (12-ounce) bag frozen cauliflower rice

1. In a small saucepan, whisk together the water, soy sauce, honey, rice vinegar, garlic powder, and ginger. Add the cornstarch and whisk until it is fully incorporated.
2. Over medium heat, bring the teriyaki sauce to a boil. Let the sauce boil for 1 minute to thicken. Remove the sauce from the heat and set aside.

3. Heat a large skillet over medium-low heat. When hot, add the oil and the chicken. Cook for 5 to 7 minutes, until the chicken is cooked through, stirring as needed.
4. Steam the broccoli and cauliflower rice in the microwave according to the package instructions.
5. Divide the cauliflower rice into four equal portions. Put one-quarter of the broccoli and chicken over each portion and top with the teriyaki sauce.

PER SERVING

Calories: 247 | Total Fat: 7g | Protein: 29g | Carbs: 20g | Sugar: 12g | Fiber: 5g | Sodium: 418mg

Coconut Lime Chicken

Prep Time: 5 minutes | Cook Time: 15 minutes | Serves 4

- 1 tablespoon coconut oil
- 4 (4-ounce) boneless, skinless chicken breasts
- ½ teaspoon salt
- 1 red bell pepper, cut into ¼-inch-thick slices
- 16 asparagus spears, bottom ends trimmed
- 1 cup unsweetened coconut milk
- 2 tablespoons freshly squeezed lime juice
- ½ teaspoon garlic powder
- ¼ teaspoon red pepper flakes
- ¼ cup chopped fresh cilantro

1. In a large skillet, heat the oil over medium-low heat. When hot, add the chicken.
2. Season the chicken with the salt. Cook for 5 minutes, then flip.
3. Push the chicken to the side of the skillet, and add the bell pepper and asparagus. Cook, covered, for 5 minutes.
4. Meanwhile, in a small bowl, whisk together the coconut milk, lime juice, garlic powder, and red pepper flakes.
5. Add the coconut milk mixture to the skillet, and boil over high heat for 2 to 3 minutes.
6. Top with the cilantro

PER SERVING

Calories: 321 | Total Fat: 19g | Protein: 30g | Carbs: 11g | Sugar: 6g | Fiber: 4g | Sodium: 378mg

Turkey Scaloppini

Prep Time: 10 minutes | Cook Time: 20 minutes | Serves 4

- ½ cup whole-wheat flour
- ½ teaspoon sea salt
- ¼ teaspoon freshly ground black pepper
- 3 tablespoons extra-virgin olive oil
- 12 ounces turkey breast, cut into ½-inch-thick cutlets and pounded flat (see headnote)
- 1 garlic clove, minced
- ½ cup dry white wine
- 2 tablespoons chopped fresh rosemary
- 1 cup low-Sodium: chicken broth
- 2 tablespoons salted butter, very cold, cut into small pieces

1. Preheat the oven to 200°F. Line a baking sheet with parchment paper.
2. In a medium bowl, whisk together the flour, salt, and pepper.
3. In a large skillet over medium-high heat, heat the olive oil until it shimmers.
4. Working in batches with one or two pieces of turkey at a time (depending on how much room you have in the pan), dredge the turkey cutlets in the flour and pat off any excess. Cook in the hot oil until the turkey is cooked through, about 3 minutes per side. Add more oil if needed.
5. Place the cooked cutlets on the lined baking sheet and keep them warm in the oven while you cook the remaining turkey and make the pan sauce.
6. Once all the turkey is cooked and warming in the oven, add the garlic to the pan and cook, stirring constantly, for 30 seconds. Add the wine and use the side of a spoon to scrape any browned bits off the bottom of the pan. Simmer, stirring, for 1 minute. Add the rosemary and chicken broth. Simmer, stirring, until it thickens, 1 to 2 minutes more.
7. Whisk in the cold butter, one piece at a time, until incorporated. Return the turkey cutlets to the sauce and turn once to coat. Serve with any remaining sauce spooned over the top.

PER SERVING

Calories: 344 | Total Fat: 20g | Saturated Fat: 7g | Sodium: 266mg | Carbs: 15g | Fiber: 2g | Protein: 24g

Ginger Beer Can Whole Chicken

Prep Time: 10 minutes | Cook Time: 50 minutes | Serves 6

- ½ cup Chicken Broth or store-bought low-Sodium: chicken broth
- 1 small yellow onion, cut into eighths
- 3 garlic cloves, smashed
- 1 (1-inch) piece fresh ginger, peeled and quartered
- 1 bay leaf
- 1 tablespoon Blackened Rub
- 1 (2-pound) whole chicken
- 1 (12-ounce) can extra-strong ginger beer

1. Preheat the oven to 375°F.
2. In a Dutch oven, bring the broth to a simmer over medium heat.
3. Add the onion, garlic, ginger, and bay leaf and cook, stirring often, for 3 to 5 minutes, or until the garlic and ginger are softened. Remove from the heat.
4. Massage the rub all over the chicken, including inside of the cavity.
5. Thoroughly wash the can of ginger beer. Open the can, and place the chicken over the can vertically.
6. Transfer the chicken to the Dutch oven, and turn on its side, allowing it to lay horizontally with the can resting inside the cavity. Cover, transfer to the oven, and cook for 45 minutes, or until the juices run clear. Discard the bay leaf.
7. Serve warm with a heaping plate of Herbed Spring Peas.

PER SERVING

Calories: 233 | Total Fat: 14g | Cholesterol: 63mg | Sodium: 61mg | Total Carbs: 8g | Sugar: 7g | Fiber: 0g | Protein: 17g

Chicken and Roasted Vegetable Wraps

Prep Time: 10 minutes | Cook Time: 20 minutes | Serves 4

- ½ small eggplant, cut into ¼-inch-thick slices
- 1 red bell pepper, seeded and cut into 1-inch-wide strips
- 1 medium zucchini, cut lengthwise into strips
- ½ small red onion, sliced
- 1 tablespoon extra-virgin olive oil
- Sea salt
- Freshly ground black pepper
- 2 (8-ounce) cooked chicken breasts, sliced
- 4 whole-wheat tortilla wraps

1. Preheat the oven to 400°F.
2. Line a baking sheet with aluminum foil and set it aside.
3. In a large bowl, toss the eggplant, bell pepper, zucchini, and red onion with the olive oil.
4. Transfer the vegetables to the baking sheet and lightly season with salt and pepper.
5. Roast the vegetables until soft and slightly charred, about 20 minutes.
6. Divide the vegetables and chicken into four portions.
7. Wrap 1 tortilla around each portion of chicken and grilled vegetables, and serve.

PER SERVING

Calories: 483 | Total Fat: 25g | Cholesterol: 46mg | Sodium: 730mg | Total Carbs: 45g | Sugar: 4g | Fiber: 3g | Protein: 20g

Kung Pao Chicken with Cashew

Prep Time: 20 minutes | **Cook Time:** 15 minutes | **Serves 4**

- 1 tablespoon of rice vinegar
- 1 tablespoon of hoisin sauce
- 1 teaspoon of chili sauce
- 1 tablespoon of cornstarch
- 1 tablespoon of tamari or soy sauce
- 1 tablespoon of ketchup
- 1/2 cup of low-Sodium: chicken or vegetable broth (chilled in the refrigerator for at least 1 hour)
- 1 tablespoon of dry sherry
- 1 red bell pepper (seeded and cut into 1-inch chunks)
- 2 scallions (white part thinly sliced and green part cut into 1-inch lengths)
- 2 tablespoons of roasted cashews
- 2 boneless chicken breasts (about 1 pound)
- ground white pepper
- 1 tablespoon of peanut oil (can use coconut or canola oil)
- 4 dried red chilies

1. Add together the cornstarch and cold broth to a glass jar with a screw-top lid. Shake vigorously until the cornstarch dissolves.
2. Add the ketchup, vinegar, hoisin sauce, tamari or soy sauce, and chili sauce to the jar. Replace the lid. Shake again until the mixture is well combined. Set it aside.
3. Slice each chicken breast in half lengthwise, then crosswise into 1/2-inch slices. Place the chicken in a bowl—season with white pepper.
4. Heat a wok or large skillet over medium-high heat, then add the oil.
5. Add the chilies and stir-fry for a few seconds, then add the chicken. Stir-fry for about 2 to 3 minutes or until the chicken starts to look opaque, then add sherry and mix well.
6. Shake the sauce in the jar, then pour it into the wok
7. Bring everything to a boil, then add the red bell pepper.
8. Stir-fry for another 2 to 3 minutes or until the chicken is cooked through and the sauce has thickened.
9. Remove from heat and stir in the scallions and cashews. Serve immediately and enjoy!

PER SERVING

Calories: 154 | Fat: 8g | Cholesterol: 83.1mg | Carbs: 14.1g | Fiber: 3.9g | Sugar: 6g | Protein: 34.8g

Ground Turkey Taco Skillet

Prep Time: 10 minutes | **Cook Time:** 20 minutes | **Serves 4**

- 3 tablespoons extra-virgin olive oil
- 1 pound ground turkey
- 1 onion, chopped
- 1 green bell pepper, seeded and chopped
- ½ teaspoon sea salt
- 1 small head cauliflower, grated
- 1 cup corn kernels
- ½ cup prepared salsa
- 1 cup shredded pepper Jack cheese

1. In a large nonstick skillet over medium-high heat, heat the olive oil until it shimmers.
2. Add the turkey. Cook, crumbling with a spoon, until browned, about 5 minutes.
3. Add the onion, bell pepper, and salt. Cook, stirring occasionally, until the vegetables soften, 4 to 5 minutes.
4. Add the cauliflower, corn, and salsa. Cook, stirring, until the cauliflower rice softens, about 3 minutes more.
5. Sprinkle with the cheese. Reduce heat to low, cover, and allow the cheese to melt, 2 or 3 minutes.

PER SERVING

Calories: 448 | Total Fat: 30g | Saturated Fat: 10g | Sodium: 649mg | Carbs: 18g | Fiber: 4g | Protein: 30g

Lemon Chicken with Rosemary and Garlic

Prep Time: 25 minutes | **Cook Time:** 20 minutes | **Serves 6**

- 2 1/2 pounds of meaty chicken pieces (breast halves, thighs, and drumsticks), skinned
- 1 tablespoon of olive oil
- 1 teaspoon of finely shredded lemon peel 1 tablespoon of lemon juice
- 1 tablespoon of snipped fresh rosemary or 1 teaspoon of dried rosemary, crushed
- 1 teaspoon of salt
- 1 teaspoon of coarsely ground black pepper
- 2 cloves garlic, minced

1. In a bowl, combine pepper, rosemary, and salt.
2. Sprinkle rosemary mixture over chicken pieces.
3. Rub in with your fingers. Place chicken pieces, bones side up in a lightly greased baking dish.
4. In another bowl, combine lemon zest, oil, lemon juice, and garlic | pour over chicken.
5. Bake at 400 degrees for about 20 minutes.
6. Turn chicken pieces bone side down | pour cooking juices over chicken.
7. Bake another 15-20 minutes or until the chicken is no longer pink. Serve and enjoy!

PER SERVING

Calories: 184, Sodium: 457mg | Protein: 25g | Cholesterol:, 77 mg Total Fat: 8g, Total Carbs: 1g

Taco Stuffed Sweet Potatoes

Prep Time: 5 minutes | Cook Time: 15 minutes | Serves 4

- 4 medium sweet potatoes
- 2 tablespoons extra-virgin olive oil
- 1 pound 93% lean ground turkey
- 2 teaspoons ground cumin
- 1 teaspoon chili powder
- ½ teaspoon salt
- ½ teaspoon freshly ground black pepper

1. Pierce the potatoes with a fork, and microwave them on the potato setting, or for 10 minutes on high power.
2. Meanwhile, heat a medium skillet over medium heat. When hot, put the oil, turkey, cumin, chili powder, salt, and pepper into the skillet, stirring and breaking apart the meat, as needed.
3. Remove the potatoes from the microwave and halve them lengthwise. Depress the centers with a spoon, and fill each half with an equal amount of cooked turkey.

PER SERVING

Calories: 300g | Total Fat: 8g | Protein: 30g | Carbs: 27g | Sugar: 4g | Fiber: 5g | Sodium: 426mg

Turkey Meatloaf Meatballs

Prep Time: 10 minutes | Cook Time: 20 minutes | Serves 4

- ¼ cup tomato paste
- 1 tablespoon honey
- 1 tablespoon Worcestershire sauce
- ½ cup milk
- ½ cup whole-wheat bread crumbs
- 1 pound ground turkey
- 1 onion, grated
- 1 tablespoon Dijon mustard
- 1 teaspoon dried thyme
- ½ teaspoon sea salt

1. Preheat the oven to 375°F. Line a rimmed baking sheet with parchment paper.
2. In a small saucepan on medium-low heat, whisk together the tomato paste, honey, and Worcestershire sauce. Bring to a simmer and then remove from the heat.
3. In a large bowl, combine the milk and bread crumbs. Let rest for 5 minutes.
4. Add the ground turkey, onion, mustard, thyme, and salt. Using your hands, mix well without overmixing.
5. Form into 1-inch meatballs and place on the prepared baking sheet. Brush the tops with the tomato paste mixture.
6. Bake until the meatballs reach 165°F internally, about 15 minutes.

PER SERVING

Calories: 285 | Total Fat: 11g | Saturated Fat: 3g | Sodium: 465mg | Carbs: 22g | Fiber: 2g | Protein: 24g

Spicy Chicken Cacciatore

Prep Time: 20 minutes | Cook Time: 1 hour | Serves 6

- 1 (2-pound) chicken
- ¼ cup all-purpose flour
- Sea salt
- Freshly ground black pepper
- 2 tablespoons extra-virgin olive oil
- 3 slices bacon, chopped
- 1 sweet onion, chopped
- 2 teaspoons minced garlic
- 4 ounces button mushrooms, halved
- 1 (28-ounce) can low-Sodium: stewed tomatoes
- ½ cup red wine
- 2 teaspoons chopped fresh oregano
- Pinch red pepper flakes

1. Cut the chicken into pieces: 2 drumsticks, 2 thighs, 2 wings, and 4 breast pieces.
2. Dredge the chicken pieces in the flour and season each piece with salt and pepper.
3. Place a large skillet over medium-high heat and add the olive oil.
4. Brown the chicken pieces on all sides, about 20 minutes in total. Transfer the chicken to a plate.
5. Add the chopped bacon to the skillet and cook until crispy, about 5 minutes. With a slotted spoon, transfer the cooked bacon to the same plate as the chicken.
6. Pour off most of the oil from the skillet, leaving just a light coating. Sauté the onion, garlic, and mushrooms in the skillet until tender, about 4 minutes.
7. Stir in the tomatoes, wine, oregano, and red pepper flakes.
8. Bring the sauce to a boil. Return the chicken and bacon, plus any accumulated juices from the plate, to the skillet.
9. Reduce the heat to low and simmer until the chicken is tender, about 30 minutes.

PER SERVING

Calories: 230 | Total Fat: 17g | Cholesterol: 25mg | Sodium: 420mg | Total Carbs: 14g | Sugar: 5g | Fiber: 2g | Protein: 8g

Chicken Enchilada Spaghetti Squash

Prep Time: 5 minutes | Cook Time: 40 minutes | Serves 4

- 1 (3-pound) spaghetti squash, halved lengthwise and seeded
- 1½ teaspoons ground cumin, divided
- Avocado oil cooking spray
- 4 (4-ounce) boneless, skinless chicken breasts
- 1 large zucchini, diced
- ¾ cup canned red enchilada sauce
- ¾ cup shredded Cheddar or mozzarella cheese

1. Preheat the oven to 400°F.
2. Season both halves of the squash with ½ teaspoon of cumin, and place them cut-side down on a baking sheet. Bake for 25 to 30 minutes.
3. Meanwhile, heat a large skillet over medium-low heat. When hot, spray the cooking surface with cooking spray and add the chicken breasts, zucchini, and 1 teaspoon of cumin. Cook the chicken for 4 to 5 minutes per side. Stir the zucchini when you flip the chicken.
4. Transfer the zucchini to a medium bowl and set aside. Remove the chicken from the skillet, and let it rest for 10 minutes or until it's cool enough to handle. Shred or dice the cooked chicken.
5. Place the chicken and zucchini in a large bowl, and add the enchilada sauce.
6. Remove the squash from the oven, flip it over, and comb through it with a fork to make thin strands.
7. Scoop the chicken mixture on top of the squash halves and top with the cheese. Return the squash to the oven and broil for 2 to 5 minutes, or until the cheese is bubbly.

PER SERVING

Calories: 331 | Total Fat: 11g | Protein: 35g | Carbs: 27g | Sugar: 2g | Fiber: 4g | Sodium: 491mg

Roasted Chicken with Tzatziki

Prep Time: 6 minutes | Cook Time: 24 minutes | Serves 4

- 4 (4-ounce) boneless, skinless chicken breasts
- Sea salt
- Freshly ground black pepper
- 1 teaspoon chopped fresh thyme, or ½ teaspoon dried thyme
- ¼ teaspoon paprika
- 1 tablespoon olive oil
- ½ cup Tzatziki Sauce, or store-bought

1. Preheat the oven to 400°F.
2. Lightly season the chicken breasts with salt and pepper, then cover them in the thyme and paprika.
3. In a large ovenproof skillet, heat the oil over medium-high heat. Brown the chicken breasts on both sides for about 4 minutes in total, turning halfway through.
4. Place the skillet in the oven and roast for about 20 minutes, until cooked through.
5. Serve the chicken breasts topped with tzatziki.

PER SERVING

Calories: 192 | Total Fat: 7g | Saturated Fat: 1g | Sodium: 112mg | Carbs: 5g | Sugar: 3g | Fiber: 1g | Protein: 27g

Ginger Citrus Chicken Thighs

Prep Time: 15 minutes | Cook Time: 30 minutes | Serves 4

- 4 chicken thighs, bone-in, skinless
- 1 tablespoon grated fresh ginger
- Sea salt
- 1 tablespoon extra-virgin olive oil
- Juice and zest of ½ lemon
- Juice and zest of ½ orange
- 2 tablespoons honey
- 1 tablespoon reduced-Sodium: soy sauce
- Pinch red pepper flakes
- 1 tablespoon chopped fresh cilantro

1. Rub the chicken thighs with the ginger and season lightly with salt.
2. Place a large skillet over medium-high heat and add the oil.
3. Brown the chicken thighs, turning once, for about 10 minutes.
4. While the chicken is browning, stir together the lemon juice and zest, orange juice and zest, honey, soy sauce, and red pepper flakes in a small bowl.
5. Add the citrus mixture to the skillet, cover, and reduce the heat to low.
6. Braise until the chicken is cooked through, about 20 minutes, adding a couple of tablespoons of water if the pan is too dry.
7. Serve garnished with the cilantro.

PER SERVING

Calories: 114 | Total Fat: 5g | Cholesterol: 34mg | Sodium: 287mg | Total Carbs: 9g | Sugar: 9g | Fiber: 0g | Protein: 9g

Chicken Salad Pitas

Prep Time: 25 minutes | Cook Time: 5 minutes | Serves 4

- 2 cups diced cooked store-bought rotisserie chicken breast
- ½ cup chopped celery
- ½ cup shredded carrot
- 1 apple, cored and chopped
- 1 scallion, both white and green parts, chopped
- ¼ cup low-fat plain Greek yogurt
- 2 tablespoons chopped cashews
- Pinch sea salt
- Pinch freshly ground black pepper
- 4 (6-inch) whole-wheat pitas, halved
- 1 cup shredded lettuce

1. In a large bowl, mix the chicken, celery, carrot, apple, scallion, yogurt, cashews, salt, and pepper until well combined.
2. Spoon the chicken mixture into the pita halves, top with lettuce, and serve 2 halves per person.

PER SERVING

Calories: 254 | Total Fat: 6g | Saturated Fat: 1g | Sodium: 233mg | Carbs: 27g | Sugar: 7g | Fiber: 4g | Protein: 24g

Lemon Chicken Piccata

Prep Time: 15 minutes | Cook Time: 30 minutes | Serves 4

- 2 tablespoons of olive oil
- 1/3 cup of lemon juice
- 1/3 cup of low Sodium: chicken stock
- 1/4 cup of drained capers
- 1/4 cup of minced Italian parsley
- 2 skinless, boneless chicken breasts
- 3 tablespoons of unsalted butter
- 1 1/2 teaspoons of all-purpose flour
- 1/4 teaspoon of white pepper
- 1/4 teaspoon of salt
- salt and pepper to taste

1. Slice each chicken breast in half lengthwise so that you get two thin slices of chicken from each breast.
2. Dip the chicken breast slices in a bit of flour seasoned with pepper and salt.
3. Heat a large skillet over medium-high heat and add the oil.
4. When the oil shimmers, add the chicken breast slices to the skillet. Cook for about 3-4 minutes per side until golden brown and cooked through. Remove the chicken slices from the skillet and set them aside.
5. Add the wine, lemon juice, and chicken stock. Increase the heat to high and simmer until the sauce thickens about 3 minutes.
6. Reduce the heat to medium and add the butter. Stir in the capers and parsley, then add the chicken to the pan to heat through.
7. Taste the sauce and adjust the seasoning.
8. Serve and enjoy!

PER SERVING

Calories: 269, Potassium 259.7mg | Protein: 20.3g | Cholesterol:, 72.6mg | Sugar: 0.4g, Total Fat: 15.6g

Turkey Taco Stuffed Sweet Potatoes

Prep Time: 15 minutes | **Cook Time:** 15 minutes | **Serves 2**

- 2 medium sweet potatoes, scrubbed and pricked with a fork
- 8 ounces ground turkey
- 2 tablespoons water
- 1 tablespoon low-Sodium: taco seasoning
- ¼ cup store-bought salsa
- ¼ cup shredded Cheddar cheese

1. Microwave the sweet potatoes for about 10 minutes, until soft.
2. While the potatoes are cooking, sauté the turkey for about 10 minutes, until cooked through. Add the water and taco seasoning and cook for 3 minutes.
3. Preheat the oven to broil.
4. Cut the sweet potatoes in half lengthwise and press them open. Scoop the turkey filling into the potatoes and top with the salsa and cheese.
5. Place the sweet potatoes in an 8-inch baking dish and broil for about 2 minutes, until the cheese is melted.
6. Serve with additional toppings (if using).

PER SERVING

Calories: 467 | Total Fat: 13g | Saturated Fat: 5g | Sodium: 324mg | Carbs: 55g | Sugar: 7g | Fiber: 7g | Protein: 30g

Turkey Meatballs

Prep Time: 10 minutes | **Cook Time:** 20 minutes | **Serves 4**

- 1 pound lean ground turkey
- ¼ cup almond flour or whole-wheat bread crumbs
- ¼ cup chopped onion
- 1 large egg
- 1 teaspoon minced garlic
- ½ teaspoon chopped fresh thyme
- ¼ teaspoon sea salt
- ⅛ teaspoon ground nutmeg
- ⅛ teaspoon freshly ground black pepper

1. Preheat the oven to 400°F. Line a baking sheet with parchment paper.
2. In a large bowl, mix the turkey, almond flour, onion, egg, garlic, thyme, salt, nutmeg, and pepper. Form the mixture into 1-inch meatballs.
3. Bake for about 20 minutes, turning halfway through, until cooked through and browned.
4. Serve with Quinoa with Chopped Pistachios or Roasted Summer Vegetables.

PER SERVING

Calories: 228 | Total Fat: 13g | Saturated Fat: 3g | Sodium: 174mg | Carbs: 3g | Sugar: 1g | Fiber: 1g | Protein: 24g

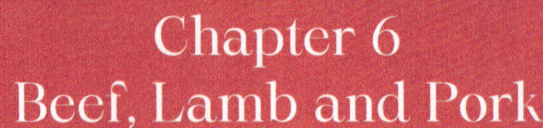

Chapter 6
Beef, Lamb and Pork

Spicy Soy Sauce in Grilled Pork Tenderloin

Prep Time: 20 minutes | Cook Time: 2 hours | Serves 6

- 1 fresh red Thai chili or cayenne chili pepper, stemmed, seeded, and minced
- 1 tablespoon of toasted sesame oil
- 1-1/2 pounds of pork tenderloin, trimmed of fat and cut into 1-inch-thick medallions
- 1/4 cup of reduced-Sodium: soy sauce
- 2 tablespoons of sugar
- 1 large clove garlic, peeled and finely grated or minced
- 1 tablespoon of finely grated fresh ginger

1. Whisk sugar and soy sauce in a bowl until sugar is completely dissolved.
2. Stir in ginger, chili, garlic,, and oil.
3. Place pork in a resealable plastic bag. Add marinade and seal bag, squeezing out the air.
4. Turn the bag over to coat the medallions.
5. Refrigerate for 2 hours, turning the bag once to redistribute the marinade.
6. Preheat grill to medium heat.
7. Remove pork from the marinade. (Discard marinade).
8. Grill medallions until just cooked through, 4 to 5 minutes per side. Serve and enjoy!

PER SERVING

Calories: 123 | Carbs: 1g | Sugar: 0.7g | Fat: 2.6g | Saturated Fat: 0.9g | Cholesterol: 73.7mg | Protein: 26.9g

Tuscan Pork Loin

Prep Time: 5 minutes | Cook Time: 55 minutes | Serves 6

- 2 tablespoons of chopped fresh rosemary
- 1 tablespoon of freshly grated lemon zest
- 2 tablespoons of white wine vinegar
- 1 3-pound of pork loin, trimmed
- 1 teaspoon of kosher salt
- 3 cloves garlic, crushed and peeled
- 2 tablespoons of extra-virgin olive oil

1. Tie kitchen string around pork in three places, so it doesn't flatten while roasting.
2. Place salt & garlic in a small bowl & mash with the back of a spoon to form a paste.
3. Stir in oil, rosemary & lemon zest. Rub the mixture into the pork. Refrigerate, uncovered, for about an hour.
4. Preheat oven to 375 degrees F.
5. Place pork in a roasting pan. Roast, turning from time to time, 40 to 50 minutes.
6. Transfer to a cutting board. Let rest for about 10 mins.
7. Meanwhile, add vermouth (or wine) and vinegar to the roasting pan and place over medium-high heat.
8. Bring to a simmer & cook, scraping up any browned bits, until the sauce is reduced by half, 2 to 4 minutes.
9. Remove the string & slice the roast.
10. Add any accumulated juices to the sauce and serve with the pork.

PER SERVING

Calories: 182 | Protein: 20.6g | Carbs: 0.6g | Dietary Fiber: 0.1g | Fat: 8.3g | Saturated Fat: 2g | Cholesterol: 64.5mg

Rice & Cuban Style Pork

Prep Time: 45 minutes | Cook Time: 1 hour | Serves 10

- 1 1/2 pounds of boneless pork chops (3/4-1 inch thick), trimmed, cut into cubes
- 2 cups of onion, chopped
- 2 cups of arborio rice or short-grain brown rice
- 2 14-ounces cans of reduced-Sodium: chicken broth
- 1 cup of canned diced tomatoes
- 1/4 teaspoon of saffron threads
- 2 cups of frozen artichoke hearts, thawed or cooked green beans, fresh or frozen, thawed
- 1/4 cup of paprika
- 1/4 cup of lime juice
- 3 tablespoons of extra-virgin olive oil, divided
- 2 tablespoons of rum (optional)
- 2 teaspoons of minced garlic, plus 2 tablespoons chopped garlic, divided
- 2 teaspoons of fresh oregano, chopped
- 1 teaspoon of kosher salt
- 1 teaspoon of freshly ground pepper
- 1/2 teaspoon of ground cumin, cumin
- 1/2 cup of roasted red peppers, cut into strips

1. Combine paprika, rum (if using), 2 teaspoons of minced garlic, oregano, salt, pepper, lime juice, 2 tablespoons of oil, and cumin in a medium bowl, stirring to make a homogeneous paste.
2. Add the pork, leaving any excess spice mixture in the bowl to add later. Cook the pork, stirring, until just cooked on the outside & the spices are very fragrant, for about 2 to 3 minutes.
3. Transfer the pork to a plate. Add onion & the rest of the 2 tablespoons of garlic to the pan. Cook, often stirring, until the onion is softened, for about 4 to 5 minutes.
4. Stir in broth, tomatoes, capers, saffron & any remaining spice mixture. (If using brown rice, also add 3/4 cup of water now.)
5. Bring to a boil, then reduce to a low simmer | cook, occasionally stirring, 15 minutes for arborio, 30 minutes for brown rice.
6. Preheat oven to 350 degrees F.
7. Stir shrimp (if using) & artichokes (or green beans) into the rice.
8. Cover and bake for 20 minutes. Stir in the pork and any accumulated juices from the plate.
9. Scatter roasted peppers on top. Cover & continue baking until the rice is tender and the liquid has been absorbed (if you've added shrimp, they should be opaque & pink) for about 10 to 15 minutes. Serve.

PER SERVING

Calories: 253 | Protein: 15.2g | Carbs: 36.2g | Dietary Fiber: 3.7g | Sugar: 3.1g | Fat: 7.9g | Saturated Fat: 1.6g;

Cheesy Beef & Noodles

Prep Time: 10 minutes | Cook Time: 15 minutes | Serves 4

- 1 lb. lean ground beef
- 1 onion, diced
- 2 cup mozzarella, grated
- ½ cup + 2 tbsp. fresh parsley diced
- Homemade Noodles, (chapter 15)
- 2 tbsp. tomato paste
- 1 tbsp. extra-virgin olive oil
- 1 tbsp. Worcestershire sauce
- 3 cloves garlic, diced fine
- 1 tsp red pepper flakes
- ½ tsp pepper
- Salt, to taste

1. Heat oil in a large skillet over med-high heat. Add beef and cook, breaking up with a spatula, about 2 minutes.
2. Reduce heat to medium and season with salt and pepper. Stir in garlic, onion, pepper flakes, Worcestershire, tomato paste, ½ cup parsley, and ½ cup water. Bring to a simmer and cook, stirring occasionally, 8 minutes.
3. Stir in noodles and cook 2 minutes more. Stir in 1 cup of cheese, sprinkle the remaining cheese over the top and cover with lid, off the heat, until cheese melts. Serve garnished with remaining parsley.

PER SERVING

Calories: 372 | Total Carbs: 7g | Net Carbs: 6g | Protein: 44g | Fat 18g | Sugar 3g | Fiber: 1g

Crust Less Pizza

Prep Time: 5 minutes | Cook Time: 25 minutes | Serves 4

- Pepperoni, ham, sausage, mushrooms, or toppings of your choice
- 8 oz. fat free cream cheese, soft
- 1 ½ cup mozzarella cheese, grated
- 2 eggs
- ½ cup lite pizza sauce
- ¼ cup reduced fat parmesan cheese
- 1 tsp garlic powder
- ¼ tsp pepper

1. Heat oven to 350 degrees. Spray and 9x13-inch baking dish with cooking spray.
2. In a large bowl, beat cream cheese, eggs, pepper, garlic powder, and parmesan until combined. Spread in prepared dish and bake 12-15 minutes or until golden brown. Let cool 10 minutes.
3. Spread pizza sauce over crust. Top with cheese and your favorite pizza toppings. Sprinkle lightly with garlic powder. Bake 8-10 minutes or until cheese melts. Cool 5 minutes before serving.

PER SERVING

Calories: 164 | Total Carbs: 4g | Net Carbs: 3g | Protein: 12g | Fat: 11g | Sugar 1g | Fiber: 1g

Creamy Braised Oxtails

Prep Time: 10 minutes | Cook Time: 4-6 hours | Serves 6

- 2 pounds oxtails
- 1 onion, diced
- ½ cup half-n-half
- 1 tsp margarine
- 1 cup low Sodium: beef broth
- ¼ cup sake
- 4 cloves garlic, diced
- 2 tbsp. chili sauce
- 1 tsp Chinese five spice
- Salt & pepper

1. Melt the margarine in a large skillet over med-high heat. Sprinkle oxtails with salt and pepper and cook until brown on all sides, about 3-4 minutes per side.
2. Add onion and garlic and cook another 3-5 minutes. Add the sake to deglaze the skillet and cook until liquid is reduced, 1-2 minutes.
3. Transfer mixture to the crock pot. Add the broth, chili sauce, and five spice, stir to combine. Cover and cook on low 6 hours, or high 4 hours, or until meat is tender.
4. Stir in the half-n-half and continue cooking another 30-60 minutes or sauce has thickened. Serve.

PER SERVING

Calories: 447 | Total Carbs: 4g | Protein: 48g | Fat: 24g | Sugar 1g | Fiber: 0g

Lamb, Mushroom, and Goat Cheese Burgers

Prep Time: 15 minutes | Cook Time: 15 minutes | Serves 4

- 8 ounces grass-fed ground lamb
- 8 ounces brown mushrooms, finely chopped
- ¼ teaspoon salt
- ¼ teaspoon freshly ground black pepper
- ¼ cup crumbled goat cheese
- 1 tablespoon minced fresh basil

1. In a large mixing bowl, combine the lamb, mushrooms, salt, and pepper, and mix well.
2. In a small bowl, mix the goat cheese and basil.
3. Form the lamb mixture into 4 patties, reserving about ½ cup of the mixture in the bowl. In each patty, make an indentation in the center and fill with 1 tablespoon of the goat cheese mixture. Use the reserved meat mixture to close the burgers. Press the meat firmly to hold together.
4. Heat the barbecue or a large skillet over medium-high heat. Add the burgers and cook for 5 to 7 minutes on each side, until cooked through. Serve.

PER SERVING

Calories: 173 | Total Fat: 13g | Protein: 11g | Carbs: 3g | Sugar: 1g | Fiber: 0g | Sodium: 154mg

Peach Salsa with Grilled Pork Tenderloin

Prep Time: 25 minutes | Cook Time: 2- minutes | Serves 4

- 1/4 teaspoon of salt
- 1/4 teaspoon of ground pepper
- 2 tablespoons of chopped fresh cilantro
- 1 tablespoon of lime juice
- 1 medium peach, halved & pitted
- 1 medium purple plum, halved & pitted
- 1 medium apricot, halved & pitted
- 1 1-inch-thick slice red onion
- 1 tablespoon of olive oil
- 1/2 teaspoon of salt
- 3/4 teaspoon of ground pepper
- 1 pound of pork tenderloin, trimmed
- 1 tablespoon of olive oil
- 2 cloves garlic, minced
- 3/4 teaspoon of chili powder
- 1/2 teaspoon of ground cumin

1. Preheat grill. Brush fruit halves and onion slice with oil. Sprinkle with a teaspoon of pepper and salt.
2. Grill the onion and fruit until tender and score from the grill for about 3 to 4 minutes per side.
3. Remove from grill and coarsely chop. Transfer to a medium bowl. Stir in cilantro & lime juice.
4. Combine cumin, oil, salt, chili powder, garlic, and pepper in a small bowl | rub over pork.
5. Grill pork over medium heat, covered, turning occasionally, about 13 to 16 minutes.
6. Transfer to a cutting board and let rest for 10 minutes.
7. Slice the pork. Divide pork slices among 4 plates and top with sauce. Serve and enjoy!

PER SERVING

Calories: 219 | Protein: 24.7g | Carbs: 8.3g | Dietary Fiber: 1.5g | Sugar: 5.7g | Fat: 9.5g | Saturated Fat: 1.8g |

Chestnut Stuffed Pork Roast

Prep Time: 15 minutes | Cook Time: 45 minutes | Serves 4

- 5 lb. pork loin roast, boneless, double tied
- ½ lb. ground pork
- ½ cup celery, diced fine
- ½ cup onion, diced fine
- 2 tbsp. fresh parsley, diced, divided
- 1 tbsp. margarine
- 15 oz. can chestnuts, drained
- 2 cup low Sodium: chicken broth
- 3 tbsp. flour
- 2 tbsp. brandy, divided
- ½ tsp salt
- ½ tsp pepper
- 1/8 tsp allspice
- Salt & black pepper, to taste

1. Heat oven to 350 degrees.
2. Untie roast, open and pound lightly to even thickness.
3. Melt margarine in a skillet over med-high heat. Add celery and onion and cook until soft.
4. In a large bowl, combine ground pork, 1 tablespoon parsley, 1 tablespoon brandy and seasonings. Mix in celery and onion. Spread over roast.
5. Lay a row of chestnuts down the center. Roll meat around filling and tie securely with butcher string. Roast in oven 1 ½ hours or until meat thermometer reaches 145 degrees. Remove and let rest 10 minutes.
6. Measure out 2 tablespoons of drippings, discard the rest, into a saucepan. Place over medium heat and whisk in flour until smooth. Add broth and cook, stirring, until mixture thickens. Chop remaining chestnuts and add to gravy along with remaining brandy and parsley. Season with salt and pepper if desired. Slice the roast and serve topped with gravy.

PER SERVING

Calories: 416 | Total Carbs: 15g | Protein: 48g | Fat: 16g | Sugar 0g | Fiber: 0g

Pork Chops with Thyme & Apple

Prep Time: 15 minutes | Cook Time: 20 minutes | Serves 4

- 1 tart apple, such as Granny Smith, peeled & sliced
- 1/4 cup of apple cider or apple juice
- 2 teaspoons of Dijon mustard
- 1/4 teaspoon of dried thyme
- 3/4 cup of reduced-Sodium: chicken broth, divided
- 2 teaspoons of cornstarch
- 2 teaspoons of canola oil
- 4 4-ounces of boneless pork chops, 1/2 inch thick, trimmed of fat
- 1 small onion, sliced

1. Mix 2 tablespoons broth and cornstarch in a small bowl.
2. Heat oil in a large nonstick skillet over high heat.
3. Add chops & cook until browned, 2 to 3 minutes per side. Transfer to a plate.
4. Reduce heat to medium-high & add onion to the pan.
5. Cook, often stirring, until it softens & browns, for about 2 to 3 minutes.
6. Add apple and cook, often stirring, until tender, for about 3 to 5 minutes.
7. Stir in the remaining broth, mustard, thyme, cider (or juice), and the cornstarch mixture.
8. Bring to a boil, stirring, until thickened and glossy, about 1 minute.
9. Return the chops to the pan. Heat through.

PER SERVING

Calories: 214 | Protein: 23.3g | Carbs: 11.4g | Dietary Fiber: 1.3g | Sugar: 8.1g | Fat: 8.2g | Saturated Fat: 2.2g | Cholesterol: 59.9mg

Pickled Onions with Raspberry Glazed Pork Chops

Prep Time: 35 minutes | **Cook Time:** 2 hours | **Serves 4**

- 4 bone-in, center-cut pork loin chops, 1/2-3/4 inch thick (1 1/2-1 3/4 pounds)
- 1/4 cup of raspberry or red-wine vinegar
- 2 teaspoons of fresh thyme leaves, divided
- 1/4 teaspoon of coarsely ground pepper, plus more to taste
- 3 cups of fresh raspberries, divided
- 1/2 cup of white wine
- 4 cups of cold water
- 2-3 small onions, thinly sliced and separated into rings (2 cups), divided
- 1/4 cup + 4-6 tablespoons of pure maple syrup, divided
- 1/4 cup + 1/4 teaspoon of kosher salt, divided
- 1 bay leaf
- 1 clove garlic, crushed
- 1 tablespoon of balsamic vinegar
- 1 tablespoon of extra-virgin olive oil

1. Combine water, 2/3 cup of onions, 1/4 cup of maple syrup, 1/4 cup of salt, bay leaf, & garlic in a large bowl or large sealable plastic bag.
2. Add pork chops | turn to combine.
3. Marinate in the refrigerator, turning the meat once or twice, for about 2 to 8 hours.
4. Whisk raspberry (or red-wine) vinegar, 2 tablespoons of maple syrup, 1 teaspoon thyme, 1/8 teaspoon of salt & pepper together in a medium bowl.
5. Add 2/3 cup of onions. Toss to coat well.
6. Refrigerate, stirring.
7. About 15 minutes before you're ready to cook the pork chops, combine 1-1/2 cups raspberries, the rest of the onions, 2 tablespoons maple syrup, wine, balsamic vinegar, and 1 teaspoon pepper in a blender.
8. Stir and press down on solids to extract all the sauce.
9. Add 1 teaspoon of thyme.
10. Remove pork chops from brine and pat dry. (Discard brine). Sprinkle both sides with 1 teaspoon salt and a generous grind of pepper.
11. Place a cast-iron skillet over medium-high heat until hot enough to sizzle a drop of water on contact.
12. Add the oil. Add the pork chops and cook until golden brown, 2 to 3 minutes per side.
13. Taste & add 1 to 2 tablespoons of maple syrup if the sauce is too tart.
14. Return the chops & any accumulated juices to the pan and cook on medium heat, turning the chops to coat with the sauce for about 2 mins until they register 145 degrees F on an instant-read thermometer.
15. Drain the pickled onions. Gently toss with the remaining 1 1/2 cups of raspberries.
16. Serve the chops with the pan sauce. Top with pickled onions & raspberries. Enjoy!

PER SERVING

Calories: 295 | Protein: 24.4g | Carbs: 21.9g | Dietary Fiber: 6.6g | Sugar: 11.1g | Fat: 11.7g | Saturated Fat: 2.5g | Cholesterol: 75mg

Crock Pot Beef Roast with Gravy

Prep Time: 15 minutes | **Cook Time:** 5 hour 30 minutes | **Serves 10**

- 3 lb. beef sirloin tip roast
- 1/4 cup lite soy sauce
- 1/4 cup water
- 3 tbsp. balsamic vinegar
- 2 tbsp. cornstarch
- 2 tbsp. coarse ground pepper
- 1 tbsp. Worcestershire sauce
- 2 tsp ground mustard
- 1½ tsp garlic, diced fine

1. Rub roast with garlic and pepper. Cut in half and place in crock pot.
2. Combine soy sauce, vinegar, Worcestershire, and mustard, pour over roast.
3. Cover and cook on low heat 5 ½-6 hours or until beef is tender.
4. Remove roast and keep warm. Strain juices into a small sauce pan, skim off fat. Heat over medium heat.
5. Stir water and cornstarch together until smooth. Stir into beef juices. Bring to a boil, and cook, stirring, 2 minutes or until thickened. Serve with roast.

PER SERVING

Calories: 264 | Total Carbs: 3g | Protein: 37g | Fat: 12g | Sugar 0g | Fiber: 0g

Curried Pork and Vegetable Kebabs

Prep Time: 15 minutes, plus 1 hour to marinate | **Cook Time:** 15 minutes | **Serves 4**

- ¼ cup plain nonfat Greek yogurt
- 2 tablespoons curry powder
- 1 teaspoon garlic powder
- 1 teaspoon ground turmeric
- Zest and juice of 1 lime
- ¼ teaspoon salt
- Pinch freshly ground black pepper
- 1 pound boneless pork tenderloin, cut into bite-size pieces
- 1 red bell pepper, seeded and cut into 2-inch squares
- 1 green bell pepper, seeded and cut into 2-inch squares
- 1 red onion, quartered and split into segments

1. In a large bowl, mix the yogurt, curry powder, garlic powder, turmeric, lime zest, lime juice, salt, and pepper.
2. Add the pieces of pork tenderloin to the bowl, and stir to coat. Refrigerate for at least 1 hour or as long as 6 hours.
3. Preheat a grill or broiler to medium.
4. Thread the pork pieces, bell peppers, and onions onto skewers.
5. Grill or broil for 12 to 15 minutes, flipping every 3 or 4 minutes, until the pork is cooked through. Serve.

PER SERVING

Calories: 175 | Total Fat: 3g | Protein: 27g | Carbs: 10g | Sugar: 4g | Fiber: 3g | Sodium: 188mg

Crock Pot Carnitas

Prep Time: 15 minutes | Cook Time: 45 minutes | Serves 4

- 4 lb. pork butt, boneless, trim the fat and cut into 2-inch cubes
- 1 onion, cut in half
- Juice from 1 orange, reserve orange halves
- 2 tbsp. fresh lime juice
- 2 cup water
- 1 ½ tsp salt
- 1 tsp cumin
- 1 tsp oregano
- 2 bay leaves
- ¾ tsp pepper

1. Place pork and orange halves in the crock pot. In a medium bowl, combine remaining Ingredients and stir to combine. Pour over pork.
2. Cover and cook on high 5 hours. Pork should be tender enough to shred with a fork. If not, cook another 60 minutes.
3. Transfer pork to a bowl. Pour the sauce into a large saucepan and discard the bay leaves and orange halves.
4. Bring to a boil and cook until it thickens and resembles a syrup.
5. Use two forks to shred the pork. Add pork to the sauce and stir to coat. Serve.

PER SERVING

Calories: 464 | Total Carbs: 3g | Protein: 35g | Fat: 35g | Sugar 1g | Fiber: 0g

Mustard-Glazed Pork Chops

Prep Time: 5 minutes | Cook Time: 25 minutes | Serves 4

- ¼ cup Dijon mustard
- 1 tablespoon pure maple syrup
- 2 tablespoons rice vinegar
- 4 bone-in, thin-cut pork chops

1. Preheat the oven to 400°F.
2. In a small saucepan, combine the mustard, maple syrup, and rice vinegar. Stir to mix and bring to a simmer over medium heat. Cook for about 2 minutes until just slightly thickened.
3. In a baking dish, place the pork chops and spoon the sauce over them, flipping to coat.
4. Bake, uncovered, for 18 to 22 minutes until the juices run clear.

PER SERVING

Calories: 257 | Total Fat: 7g | Protein: 39g | Carbs: 7g | Sugar: 4g | Fiber: 0g | Sodium: 466mg

Quick Bison Meatballs

Prep Time: 10 minutes | Cook Time: 10 minutes | Serves 2

- Ground bison – 8 pounds
- Egg – 1
- Garlic (finely chopped) – 2 cloves
- Feta cheese (fat-free) – 0.4 cup
- Onion powder – 1 tablespoon
- Parsley (chopped) – 1 tablespoon
- Dried oregano – 1 tablespoon
- Salt – as per taste
- Pepper – as per taste

1. Start by taking a large mixing bowl and adding in the ground bison.
2. Add the finely chopped garlic, spices, and eggs to the bison. Mix well to combine.
3. Add in the feta and use your hands to gently fold it into the bison mix.
4. Divide the bison and feta mixture into 10 equal portions. Roll each portion into a ball.
5. Take a shallow skillet and grease it using cooking spray. Place the skillet over a medium flame.
6. Once the skillet is heated through, place the meatballs into it and let them cook for around 7 minutes. Keep turning them to cook them evenly on each side.
7. Once done, transfer the meatballs into a serving platter. Serve with salad, pita bread, or tzatziki.

PER SERVING

Calories: 271 | Fat: 13.5 g | Protein: 33.7 g | Carbs: 2.8 g

Parmesan-Crusted Pork Chops

Prep Time: 10 minutes | Cook Time: 25 minutes | Serves 4

- Nonstick cooking spray
- 4 bone-in, thin-cut pork chops
- 2 tablespoons butter
- ½ cup grated Parmesan cheese
- 3 garlic cloves, minced
- ¼ teaspoon salt
- ¼ teaspoon dried thyme
- Freshly ground black pepper

1. Preheat the oven to 400°F. Line a baking sheet with parchment paper and spray with nonstick cooking spray.
2. Arrange the pork chops on the prepared baking sheet so they do not overlap.
3. In a small bowl, combine the butter, cheese, garlic, salt, thyme, and pepper. Press 2 tablespoons of the cheese mixture onto the top of each pork chop.
4. Bake for 18 to 22 minutes until the pork is cooked through and its juices run clear. Set the broiler to high, then broil for 1 to 2 minutes to brown the tops.

PER SERVING

Calories: 332 | Total Fat: 16g | Protein: 44g | Carbs: 1g | Sugar: 0g | Fiber: 0g | Sodium: 440mg

Mango-Glazed Pork Tenderloin Roast

Prep Time: 10 minutes | Cook Time: 20 minutes | Serves 4

- 1 pound boneless pork tenderloin, trimmed of fat
- 1 teaspoon chopped fresh rosemary
- 1 teaspoon chopped fresh thyme
- ¼ teaspoon salt, divided
- ¼ teaspoon freshly ground black pepper, divided
- 1 teaspoon extra-virgin olive oil
- 1 tablespoon honey
- 2 tablespoons white wine vinegar
- 2 tablespoons dry cooking wine
- 1 tablespoon minced fresh ginger
- 1 cup diced mango

1. Preheat the oven to 400°F.
2. Season the tenderloin with the rosemary, thyme, ⅛ teaspoon of salt, and ⅛ teaspoon of pepper.
3. Heat the olive oil in an oven-safe skillet over medium-high heat, and sear the tenderloin until browned on all sides, about 5 minutes total.
4. Transfer the skillet to the oven and roast for 12 to 15 minutes until the pork is cooked through, the juices run clear, and the internal temperature reaches 145°F. Transfer to a cutting board to rest for 5 minutes.
5. In a small bowl, combine the honey, vinegar, cooking wine, and ginger. In to the same skillet, pour the honey mixture and simmer for 1 minute. Add the mango and toss to coat. Transfer to a blender and purée until smooth. Season with the remaining ⅛ teaspoon of salt and ⅛ teaspoon of pepper.
6. Slice the pork into rounds and serve with the mango sauce.

PER SERVING

Calories: 182 | Total Fat: 4g | Protein: 24g | Carbs: 12g | Sugar: 10g | Fiber: 1g | Sodium: 240mg

Roasted Veggies with Flank Steak

Prep Time: 20 minutes | Cook Time: 20 minutes | Serves 6

- Flank steak – 1.5 ounces
- Lime juice – ¼ cup
- Garlic (minced) – 1 clove
- Ground ginger – ½ tablespoon
- Red pepper flakes – ¼ teaspoon
- Cumin – ¼ teaspoon
- Salt – ½ teaspoon
- Pepper – ¼ teaspoon
- Mushrooms (sliced) – 8 ounces
- Grape tomatoes (halved) – 300 g
- Zucchini (cubed) – 1
- Coconut oil (melted) – 1 tablespoon
- Cilantro (chopped) – 2 teaspoons
- Lime juice – 2 tablespoons
- Salt – ¼ teaspoon
- Pepper – ¼ teaspoon

1. Start by taking a medium-sized mixing bowl. Add in the garlic, cumin, ginger, chili flakes, lime juice, pepper, and salt. Mix well to combine. Your marinade is ready.
2. Take a gallon zip-lock bag and place the flank steak inside it. Pour the marinade on the steak and seal the bag. Mix until the steak is fully covered.
3. Place the flank steak in the refrigerator and let it sit for about 30 minutes.
4. Set the temperature of the oven to 400°F and let it preheat.
5. Take a large baking sheet and place the mushrooms, zucchini, and tomatoes on it. Pour coconut oil on top and ensure the veggies are evenly covered.
6. Sprinkle pepper, salt, lime juice, and cilantro on top of the veggies. Mix well.
7. Place the baking sheet in the preheated oven and roast for about 10 minutes. Toss the veggies and roast for another 10 minutes.
8. In the meantime, let the grill preheat.
9. Take the flank steak out of the fridge and remove it from the bag. Place it on the preheated grill.
10. Grill the flank steak for about 10 minutes. Flip over and grill for another 10 minutes.
11. Once done, let it rest on a rack for about 10 minutes.
12. Slice the flank steak into ½-inch-thick slices and place the roasted veggies on top.
13. Serve hot!

PER SERVING

Calories: 241 | Fat: 11.5 g | Protein: 26.6 g | Carbs: 8.3 g

Chapter 7
Fish and Seafood

Tuna and Avocado Salad

Prep Time: 5 minutes | Cook Time: 5 minutes | Serves 4

- Canned tuna (drained) – 10 ounces
- Avocado – 1 large
- Celery rib – 1
- Fresh garlic – 2 cloves
- Mayonnaise – 3 tablespoons
- Red onion (peeled) – 1 small
- Lemon juice (freshly squeezed) – 1 tablespoon
- Cucumber – ¼
- Parsley – 1 handful
- Salt – ¼ teaspoon
- Pepper – as per taste

1. Start by rinsing the cucumber, onion, celery, and parsley. Dry using a kitchen towel.
2. Finely chop the onion, celery, and cucumber. Also, very finely mince the garlic cloves. (You can use a garlic press, if handy.)
3. Take the avocado and cut it into 2 halves. Use a spoon to scoop out the pulp. Dice it into small pieces
4. Take a salad mixing bowl and add in half of the parsley, chopped onion, cucumber, celery, and minced garlic. Toss using a spoon.
5. Now add in the diced avocado and mayonnaise. Gently fold until all the ingredients are well-coated.
6. Season with pepper and salt as per your liking. Give the salad a gentle toss.
7. Serve in a bowl and garnish with reserved fresh parsley!

PER SERVING

Calories: 225 | Fat: 16.3 g | Protein: 13.9 g | Carbs: 7.1 g

Greens Shrimp Salad

Prep Time: 10 minutes | Cook Time: 6 minutes | Serves 1

- 1 tablespoon olive oil
- ½ of garlic clove, crushed
- ¼ pound shrimp, peeled and deveined
- Salt and black pepper, to taste
- ¾ cup baby arugula
- ¾ cup baby spinach
- ¼ tablespoon lime juice

1. In a suitable wok, heat the oil over medium heat and sauté garlic for almost 1 minute. Add the shrimp with salt and black pepper and cook for almost 3-5 minutes. Remove it from the heat and set it aside to cool.
2. In a salad bowl, add the shrimp, arugula, spinach, remaining oil, lime juice, salt and black pepper and gently toss to coat. Serve immediately.

PER SERVING

Calories: 266 | Fat: 14.5g | Total Carbs: 3.6g | Fiber: 0.8g | Sugar: 0.4g | Net Carbs: 2g | Protein: 27g

Tuna Egg Salad

Prep Time: 10 minutes | Cook Time: 10 minutes | Serves 1

- ½ tablespoon dill, minced
- ½ tablespoon olive oil
- ¼ tablespoon lime juice
- Salt and black pepper, to taste
- 1 cup spinach, torn
- 3 ounces canned water-packed tuna, drained and flaked
- 1 hard-boiled egg, peeled and sliced
- ¼ cup tomato, chopped

1. For the dressing: place dill, oil, lime juice, salt, and black pepper in a suitable bowl and beat until well combined. Place the torn spinach onto a serving plate and top with tuna, egg and tomato.
2. Drizzle with dressing and serve.

PER SERVING

Calories: 241 | Fat: 12.4g | Total Carbs: 4.1g | Fiber: 1.4g | Sugar: 1.7g | Net Carbs: 2g | Protein: 28.8g

Avocado Shrimp Salad

Prep Time: 10 minutes | Cook Time: 10 minutes | Serves 1

- ½ tablespoon olive oil
- ½ tablespoon lime juice
- ¼ teaspoon ground cumin
- Salt, as required
- ¼ pound cooked shrimp
- ½ of a small avocado, peeled, pitted and cubed
- ½ of scallion, chopped

1. For the dressing: in a salad bowl, add oil, lime juice, cumin and salt and beat until well combined.
2. In the salad bowl, add shrimp, avocado and scallion and gently toss to coat well. Serve immediately.

PER SERVING

Calories: 285 | Fat: 15.5g | Total Carbs: 7.5g | Fiber: 4.1g | Sugar: 0.5g | Net Carbs: 5g | Protein: 27.1g

Shrimp Cocktail

Prep Time: 15 minutes | Cook Time: 3 minutes | Serves 4

- 1 pound (454 g) medium shrimp, peeled and deveined
- 1 cup diced mango
- 2 ripe avocados, diced
- ¼ cup finely diced red onion
- 2 Roma tomatoes, diced
- ¼ cup chopped fresh cilantro
- 2 tablespoons low-carb tomato ketchup
- Juice of 1 lime
- Juice of 1 orange
- 1 tablespoon extra-virgin olive oil
- 1 jalapeño pepper, seeded and minced
- Lime wedges, for serving

1. Fill a large pot about halfway with water and bring to a boil. Meanwhile, fill a large bowl ⅔ of the way with ice and about 1 cup of cold water.
2. Add the shrimp to the boiling water and cook for 3 minutes until they are opaque and firm. Drain and quickly transfer to the ice water bath for 3 minutes to stop the cooking and cool them. Drain and pat the shrimp dry with a clean paper towel.
3. In a large bowl, mix together the shrimp, mango, avocado, red onion, tomatoes, and cilantro.
4. In a small bowl, combine the ketchup, lime juice, orange juice, oil, and jalapeño. Mix well and gently fold the sauce into the shrimp mixture.
5. Divide among 4 glasses or small dishes, with a lime wedge on the rim of each.

PER SERVING

Calories: 278 | Fat: 16.1g | Protein: 17.9g | Carbs: 20.1g | Fiber: 6.1g | Sugar: 9.9g | Sodium: 675mg

Easy Crab Cakes

Prep Time: 10 minutes | Cook Time: 10 minutes | Serves 1

- ¾ tablespoon olive oil
- 2 tablespoons onion, chopped
- ¾ tablespoon blanched almond flour
- 1 tablespoon egg white
- ½ tablespoon low-fat mayonnaise
- ¼ tablespoon dried parsley, crushed
- ¼ teaspoon yellow mustard
- ¼ teaspoon Worcestershire sauce, low-Sodium:
- ¼ tablespoon old bay seasoning
- black pepper, to taste
- ¼ lb. lump crabmeat, drained

1. Heat up a teaspoon of olive oil in a wok over medium heat and sauté onion for almost 8-10 minutes. Remove the frying pan from heat and set it aside to cool slightly.
2. Place cooked onion and remaining ingredients except for crabmeat in a suitable mixing bowl and mix until well combined. In the bowl of onion mixture, add the crabmeat and gently stir to combine. Make 2 equal-sized patties from the mixture. Arrange the patties onto a foil-lined tray and refrigerate for almost 30 minutes.
3. In a large frying pan, heat the remaining oil over medium-low heat and cook the crab patties for almost 3-4 minutes per side or until desired doneness. Serve hot.

PER SERVING

Calories: 253 | Fat: 19g | Total Carbs: 5.1g | Fiber: 1.1g | Sugar: 1.9g | Net Carbs: 5g | Protein: 15.6g

Green Salmon Florentine

Prep Time: 10 minutes | Cook Time: 30 minutes | Serves 4

- 1 teaspoon extra-virgin olive oil
- ½ sweet onion, finely chopped
- 1 teaspoon minced garlic
- 3 cups baby spinach
- 1 cup kale, tough stems removed, torn into 3-inch pieces
- Sea salt and freshly ground black pepper, to taste
- 4 (5-ounce / 142-g) salmon fillets
- Lemon wedges, for serving

1. Preheat the oven to 350°F (180°C).
2. Place a large skillet over medium-high heat and add the oil.
3. Sauté the onion and garlic until softened and translucent, about 3 minutes.
4. Add the spinach and kale and sauté until the greens wilt, about 5 minutes.
5. Remove the skillet from the heat and season the greens with salt and pepper.
6. Place the salmon fillets so they are nestled in the greens and partially covered by them. Bake the salmon until it is opaque, about 20 minutes.
7. Serve immediately with a squeeze of fresh lemon.

PER SERVING

Calories: 282 | Fat: 15.9g | Protein: 28.9g | Carbs: 4.1g | Fiber: 1.1g | Sugar: 0.9g | Sodium: 92mg

Corn Shrimp Salad

Prep Time: 10 minutes | Cook Time: 10 minutes | Serves 4

- ¼ pound cooked shrimp
- 1 cup lettuce, torn
- 2 tablespoons onion, sliced
- ¼ tablespoon olive oil
- Salt and black pepper, to taste

1. In a salad bowl, add shrimp, corn, onion, oil, salt and black pepper and toss to coat well.
2. Serve immediately.

PER SERVING

Calories: 180 | Fat: 5.5g | Total Carbs: 5.1g | Fiber: 0.8g | Sugar: 1.4g | Net Carbs: 2g | Protein: 26.3g

Shrimp Olives Salad

Prep Time: 10 minutes | Cook Time: 3 minutes | Serves 1

- ¼ pound shrimp, peeled and deveined
- 1 lemon slice
- ½ tablespoon olive oil
- ½ teaspoon lemon juice
- Salt and black pepper, to taste
- ½ of tomato, sliced
- 1 tablespoon onion, sliced
- 1 tablespoon green olives
- 1 teaspoon parsley, chopped

1. In a small pan of lightly salted boiling water, add the lemon slice. Then, add the shrimp and cook for almost 2-3 minutes or until pink and opaque.
2. With a slotted spoon, transfer the shrimp into a suitable bowl of ice water to stop the cooking process. Drain the shrimp completely, and then pat dry with paper towels.
3. In a suitable bowl, add the oil, lemon juice, salt, and black pepper, and beat until well combined. Place the shrimp, tomato, onion, olives, and parsley onto a serving plate. Drizzle with oil mixture and serve.

PER SERVING

Calories: 215 | Fat: 9.9g | Total Carbs: 4.5g | Fiber: 0.9g | Sugar: 1.3g | Net Carbs: 4g | Protein: 26.3g

Tuna Cucumber Salad

Prep Time: 10 minutes | Cook Time: 10 minutes | Serves 1

- 1 tablespoon extra-virgin olive oil
- ½ tablespoon lime juice
- ¼ teaspoon Dijon mustard
- ⅛ teaspoon lime zest, grated
- Salt and black pepper, to taste
- 3 ounces canned water-packed tuna, drained and flaked
- ¼ of cucumber, sliced
- 1 tablespoon red onion, chopped
- ¼ of tomato, sliced
- 1 cup lettuce leaves, torn

1. In a suitable bowl, add all the recipe ingredients and beat until well combined.
2. In a large serving bowl, add all the recipe ingredients and mix. Place the dressing over the salad and gently toss to coat. Refrigerate, covered for almost 30-40 minutes before serving.

PER SERVING

Calories: 246 | Fat: 15g | Total Carbs: 6.1g | Fiber: 1.2g | Sugar: 2.7g | Net Carbs: 5g | Protein: 22.6g

Shrimp and Jalapeno Veggie Bake

Prep Time: 20 minutes | Cook Time: 35 minutes | Serves 4

- Shrimp – medium (peeled and thawed) – 15
- Red onion (sliced) – 1/4 cup
- Tomato (sliced) – 1 large
- Zucchini (sliced) – 2
- Jalapeño (deseeded and sliced) – 1
- Cream – 1/3 cup
- Eggs – 2
- Melted butter – 1 tablespoon
- Garlic (minced) – 2 cloves
- Starch (gluten-free) – ¼ cup
- Sea salt – as per taste
- Black pepper – as per taste
- Parmesan (grated) – ½ cup
- Chili flakes – ½ teaspoon
- Olive oil spray
- Cilantro (chopped) – for garnishing
- Chili flakes – for garnishing

1. Start by preheating the oven to 350°F.
2. Take a cast-iron pan and lightly grease it using olive oil spray. Layer the bottom of the pan with the onion, tomato, zucchini. and jalapeno.
3. Layer the shrimps on top of the vegetables.
4. Take a small mixing bowl and add in garlic, starch, cream, egg, and melted butter. Whisk well until the mixture is smooth.
5. Pour the cream and egg mixture over the shrimps and veggies. Season with pepper and salt as per your taste.
6. Top the shrimps with ½ cup of grated parmesan and finish by sprinkling chili flakes.
7. Place the cast-iron pan in the oven and let the shrimps and veggies bake for about 40 minutes.
8. Once done, take the pan out of the oven and season with more pepper and salt.
9. Garnish with chopped cilantro and chili flakes. Serve hot!

PER SERVING

Calories: 240 | Fat: 9 g | Protein: 20 g | Carbs: 8 g

Crab Cakes with Salsa

Prep Time: 15 minutes | **Cook Time:** 45 minutes | **Serves 4**

- 1 cup finely chopped honeydew melon
- 1 scallion, white and green parts, finely chopped
- 1 red bell pepper, seeded, finely chopped
- 1 teaspoon chopped fresh thyme
- Pinch sea salt
- Pinch freshly ground black pepper
- 1 pound (454 g) lump crabmeat, drained and picked over
- ¼ cup finely chopped red onion
- ¼ cup panko bread crumbs
- 1 tablespoon chopped fresh parsley
- 1 teaspoon lemon zest
- 1 egg
- ¼ cup whole-wheat flour
- Nonstick cooking spray

1. In a small bowl, stir together the melon, scallion, bell pepper, and thyme.
2. Season the salsa with salt and pepper and set aside.
3. In a medium bowl, mix together the crab, onion, bread crumbs, parsley, lemon zest, and egg until very well combined.
4. Divide the crab mixture into 8 equal portions and form them into patties about ¾-inch thick.
5. Chill the crab cakes in the refrigerator for at least 1 hour to firm them up.
6. Dredge the chilled crab cakes in the flour until lightly coated, shaking off any excess flour.
7. Place a large skillet over medium heat and lightly coat it with cooking spray.
8. Cook the crab cakes until they are golden brown, turning once, about 5 minutes per side.
9. Serve warm with the salsa.

PER SERVING

Calories: 233 | Fat: 3.1g | Protein: 31.9g | Carbs: 18.1g | Fiber: 2.1g | Sugar: 6.1g | Sodium: 770mg

Hearty Faux Conch Fritters

Prep Time: 15 minutes | **Cook Time:** 20 minutes | **Serves 4**

- 4 medium egg whites
- ½ cup fat-free milk
- 1 cup chickpea crumbs
- ¼ teaspoon freshly ground black pepper
- ½ teaspoon ground cumin
- 3 cups frozen chopped scallops, thawed
- 1 small onion, finely chopped
- 1 small green bell pepper, finely chopped
- 2 celery stalks, finely chopped
- 2 garlic cloves, minced
- Juice of 2 limes

1. Preheat the oven to 350°F (180°C).
2. In a large bowl, combine the egg whites, milk, and chickpea crumbs.
3. Add the black pepper and cumin and mix well.
4. Add the scallops, onion, bell pepper, celery, and garlic.
5. Form golf ball–size patties and place on a rimmed baking sheet 1 inch apart.
6. Transfer the baking sheet to the oven and cook for 5 to 7 minutes, or until golden brown.
7. Flip the patties, return to the oven, and bake for 5 to 7 minutes, or until golden brown.
8. Top with the lime juice, and serve.

PER SERVING

Calories: 338 | Fat: 0g | Protein: 50.1g | Carbs: 24.1g | Fiber: 5.9g | Sugar: 4.0g | Sodium: 465mg

Chapter 8
Vegetable and Side Dishes

Crispy Parmesan Cups with White Beans and Veggies

Prep Time: 10 minutes | Cook Time: 5 minutes | Serves 4

- 1 cup grated Parmesan cheese, divided
- 1 (15-ounce) can low-Sodium: white beans, drained and rinsed
- 1 cucumber, peeled and finely diced
- ½ cup finely diced red onion
- ¼ cup thinly sliced fresh basil
- 1 garlic clove, minced
- ½ jalapeño pepper, diced
- 1 tablespoon extra-virgin olive oil
- 1 tablespoon balsamic vinegar
- ¼ teaspoon salt
- Freshly ground black pepper

1. Heat a medium nonstick skillet over medium heat. Sprinkle 2 tablespoons of cheese in a thin circle in the center of the pan, flattening it with a spatula.
2. When the cheese melts, use a spatula to flip the cheese and lightly brown the other side.
3. Remove the cheese "pancake" from the pan and place into the cup of a muffin tin, bending it gently with your hands to fit in the muffin cup.
4. Repeat with the remaining cheese until you have 8 cups.
5. In a mixing bowl, combine the beans, cucumber, onion, basil, garlic, jalapeño, olive oil, and vinegar, and season with the salt and pepper.
6. Fill each cup with the bean mixture just before serving.

PER SERVING

Calories: 259 | Total Fat: 12g | Protein: 15g | Carbs: 24g | Sugar: 4g | Fiber: 8g | Sodium: 551mg

Brussels Sprout, Avocado, and Wild Rice Bowl

Prep Time: 15 minutes | Cook Time: 15 minutes | Serves 4

- 2 cups sliced Brussels sprouts
- 2 teaspoons extra-virgin olive oil, plus 2 tablespoons
- Juice of 1 lemon
- 1 teaspoon Dijon mustard
- 1 garlic clove, minced
- ½ teaspoon salt
- ¼ teaspoon freshly ground black pepper
- 1 cup cooked wild rice
- 1 cup sliced radishes
- 1 avocado, sliced

1. Preheat the oven to 400°F. Line a baking sheet with parchment paper.
2. In a medium bowl, toss the Brussels sprouts with 2 teaspoons of olive oil and spread on the prepared baking sheet. Roast for 12 minutes, stirring once, until lightly browned.
3. In a small bowl, mix the remaining 2 tablespoons of olive oil, lemon juice, mustard, garlic, salt, and pepper.
4. In a large bowl, toss the cooked wild rice, radishes, and roasted Brussels sprouts. Drizzle the dressing

over the salad and toss.
5. Divide among 4 bowls and top with avocado slices.

PER SERVING

Calories: 178 | Total Fat: 11g | Protein: 2g | Carbs: 18g | Sugar: 2g | Fiber: 5g | Sodium: 299mg

Hoppin John

Prep Time: 15 minutes | Cook Time: 50 minutes | Serves 12

- 1 tablespoon canola oil
- 2 celery stalks, thinly sliced
- 1 small yellow onion, chopped
- 1 medium green bell pepper, chopped
- 1 tablespoon tomato paste
- 2 garlic cloves, minced
- 2 cups brown rice, rinsed
- 5 cups Vegetable Broth (here) or store-bought low-Sodium: vegetable broth, divided
- 2 bay leaves
- 1 teaspoon smoked paprika
- 1 teaspoon Creole Seasoning
- 1¼ cups frozen black-eyed peas

1. In a Dutch oven, heat the canola oil over medium heat.
2. Add the celery, onion, bell pepper, tomato paste, and garlic and cook, stirring often, for 3 to 5 minutes, or until the vegetables are softened.
3. Add the rice, 4 cups of broth, bay leaves, paprika, and Creole seasoning.
4. Reduce the heat to low, cover, and cook for 30 minutes, or until the rice is tender.
5. Add the black-eyed peas and remaining 1 cup of broth. Mix well, cover, and cook for 12 minutes, or until the peas soften. Discard the bay leaves.
6. Enjoy with Broccoli Stalk Slaw.

PER SERVING

Calories: 149 | Total Fat: 2g | Cholesterol: 0mg | Sodium: 37mg | Total Carbs: 28g | Sugar: 1g | Fiber: 2g | Protein: 4g

Red Beans

Prep Time: 10 minutes | Cook Time: 45 minutes | Serves 8

- 1 cup crushed tomatoes
- 1 medium yellow onion, chopped
- 2 garlic cloves, minced
- 2 cups dried red kidney beans
- 1 cup roughly chopped green beans
- 4 cups Vegetable Broth (here) or store-bought low-Sodium: vegetable broth
- 1 teaspoon smoked paprika

1. Select the Sauté setting on an electric pressure cooker, and combine the tomatoes, onion, and garlic. Cook for 3 to 5 minutes, or until softened.
2. Add the kidney beans, green beans, broth, and paprika. Stir to combine.
3. Close and lock the lid, and set the pressure valve to sealing.
4. Change to the Manual/Pressure Cook setting, and cook for 35 minutes.
5. Once cooking is complete, quick-release the pressure. Carefully remove the lid.
6. Serve with Veggie Unfried Rice.

PER SERVING

Calories: 187 | Total Fat: 1g | Cholesterol: 0mg | Sodium: 102mg | Total Carbs: 34g | Sugar: 4g | Fiber: 10g | Protein: 13g

Easy Pad Thai

Prep Time: 5 minutes | Cook Time: 20 minutes | Serves 4

- Avocado oil cooking spray
- 4 cups carrot noodles
- 4 cups fresh broccoli florets
- 3 ounces extra-firm tofu, cut to ½-inch cubes
- ⅔ cup Thai-Style Peanut Sauce
- ½ cup chopped unsalted peanuts

1. Heat a large skillet over medium-low heat. When hot, coat the cooking surface with cooking spray. Put the carrot noodles and broccoli in the skillet, and cook for 10 minutes, covered.
2. Meanwhile, press the tofu between layers of paper towels to remove any excess moisture. Be sure not to break or crumble the tofu.
3. Heat another skillet over medium heat. When hot, coat the cooking surface with cooking spray. Put the tofu in the skillet, and cook for 2 minutes on each side, until golden brown.
4. When the vegetables are tender, add the peanut sauce and toss. Divide the vegetable mixture into four equal portions, and top each portion with one-quarter of the tofu.
5. Top with the chopped peanuts and scallions (if using).

PER SERVING

Calories: 419 | Total Fat: 31g | Protein: 18g | Carbs: 25g | Sugar: 11g | Fiber: 10g | Sodium: 323mg

Beet Greens and Black Beans

Prep Time: 10 minutes | Cook Time: 20 minutes | Serves 4

- 1 tablespoon unsalted non-hydrogenated plant-based butter
- ½ Vidalia onion, thinly sliced
- ½ cup Vegetable Broth (here) or store-bought low-Sodium: vegetable broth
- 1 bunch beet greens, cut into ribbons
- 1 bunch dandelion greens, cut into ribbons
- 1 (15-ounce) can no-salt-added black beans
- Freshly ground black pepper

1. In a medium skillet, melt the butter over low heat.
2. Add the onion, and sauté for 3 to 5 minutes, or until the onion is translucent.
3. Add the broth and greens. Cover the skillet and cook for 7 to 10 minutes, or until the greens are wilted.
4. Add the black beans and cook for 3 to 5 minutes, or until the beans are tender. Season with black pepper.

PER SERVING

Calories: 161 | Total Fat: 4g | Cholesterol: 0mg | Sodium: 224mg | Total Carbs: 26g | Sugar: 1g | Fiber: 10g | Protein: 9g

Edamame Peanut Bowl

Prep Time: 5 minutes | Cook Time: 15 minutes | Serves 4

- 2 cups frozen broccoli florets
- 2 cups frozen cauliflower florets
- 1 cup frozen shelled edamame
- 2 cups carrot noodles
- ½ cup Thai-Style Peanut Sauce

1. Heat a large skillet over medium-high heat. When hot, add the broccoli, cauliflower, edamame, and carrot noodles, and cover. Cook for 3 to 5 minutes.
2. Uncover and cook until any water evaporates completely. The bottom of the pan should be dry when you stir.
3. Divide the vegetables into four equal portions, and top each serving with 2 tablespoons of peanut sauce.

PER SERVING

Calories: 283 | Total Fat: 15g | Protein: 12g | Carbs: 25g | Sugar: 10g | Fiber: 10g | Sodium: 172mg

Savory Bread Pudding with Mushrooms and Kale

Prep Time: 20 minutes | Cook Time: 35 minutes | Serves 2

- 1 large egg
- ½ cup 2% milk
- ½ teaspoon Dijon mustard
- Pinch freshly grated nutmeg
- Pinch kosher salt
- Pinch freshly ground black pepper
- 1 slice sourdough bread (about 1 ounce), cut into 1-inch cubes
- 1 tablespoon avocado oil
- ¼ cup chopped onion
- 2 ounces mushrooms, sliced (about 3 creminis)
- ¼ teaspoon dried thyme
- 1 cup chopped lacinato kale, stems and ribs removed (from 2 stems)
- Nonstick cooking spray
- ¼ cup grated Gruyère cheese
- 1 tablespoon shredded Parmesan

1. In a 2-cup measuring cup with a spout, whisk together the egg, milk, mustard, nutmeg, salt, and pepper. Add the bread and submerge it in the liquid.
2. Set the electric pressure cooker to the Sauté setting. When the pot is hot, pour in the avocado oil.
3. Add the onion, mushrooms, and thyme to the pot and sauté for 3 to 5 minutes or until the onion begins to soften. Stir in the kale and cook for about 2 minutes or until it wilts. Hit Cancel.
4. Spray the ramekins with cooking spray. Divide the mushroom mixture between the ramekins. Top each with 2 tablespoons Gruyère. Pour half of the egg mixture into each ramekin and stir. Make sure the bread stays submerged. Cover with foil.
5. Pour 1 cup of water into the electric pressure cooker and insert a wire rack or trivet. Place the ramekins on the rack.
6. Close and lock the lid of the pressure cooker. Set the valve to sealing.
7. Cook on high pressure for 8 minutes.
8. When the cooking is complete, hit Cancel. Allow the pressure to release naturally for 10 minutes, then quick release any remaining pressure.
9. Using tongs or the handles of the rack, transfer the ramekins to a cutting board. Carefully lift the foil and sprinkle the Parmesan on top. Replace the foil for about 5 minutes or until the cheese melts.
10. Remove the foil and serve immediately.

PER SERVING

Calories: 295 | Total Fat: 17g | Protein: 13g | Carbs: 23g | Sugar: 7g | Fiber: 3g | Sodium: 313mg

Mexican Zucchini Casserole

Prep Time: 10 minutes | Cook Time: 45 minutes | Serves 4

- 1 (6 to 7-inch) zucchini, trimmed
- Nonstick cooking spray
- 1 (15-ounce) can pinto beans or 1½ cups Salt-Free No-Soak Beans, rinsed and drained
- 1⅓ cups salsa
- 1⅓ cups shredded Mexican cheese blend

1. Slice the zucchini into rounds. You'll need at least 16 slices.
2. Spray a 6-inch cake pan with nonstick spray.
3. Put the beans into a medium bowl and mash some of them with a fork.
4. Cover the bottom of the pan with about 4 zucchini slices. Add about ⅓ of the beans, ⅓ cup of salsa, and ⅓ cup of cheese. Press down. Repeat for 2 more layers. Add the remaining zucchini, salsa, and cheese. (There are no beans in the top layer.)
5. Cover the pan loosely with foil.
6. Pour 1 cup of water into the electric pressure cooker.
7. Place the pan on the wire rack and carefully lower it into the pot. Close and lock the lid of the pressure cooker. Set the valve to sealing.
8. Cook on high pressure for 15 minutes.
9. When the cooking is complete, hit Cancel and allow the pressure to release naturally.
10. Once the pin drops, unlock and remove the lid.
11. Carefully remove the pan from the pot, lifting by the handles of the wire rack. Let the casserole sit for 5 minutes before slicing into quarters and serving.

PER SERVING

Calories: 252 | Total Fat: 12g | Protein: 16g | Carbs: 23g | Sugar: 4g | Fiber: 7g | Sodium: 1089mg

Stuffed Portobello Mushrooms

Prep Time: 5 minutes | Cook Time: 20 minutes | Serves 4

- 8 large portobello mushrooms
- 3 teaspoons extra-virgin olive oil, divided
- 4 cups fresh spinach
- 1 medium red bell pepper, diced
- ¼ cup crumbled feta

1. Preheat the oven to 450°F.
2. Remove the stems from the mushrooms, and gently scoop out the gills and discard. Coat the mushrooms with 2 teaspoons of olive oil.
3. On a baking sheet, place the mushrooms cap-side down, and roast for 20 minutes.
4. Meanwhile, heat the remaining 1 teaspoon of olive oil in a medium skillet over medium heat. When hot, sauté the spinach and red bell pepper for 8 to 10 minutes, stirring occasionally.
5. Remove the mushrooms from the oven. Drain, if necessary. Spoon the spinach and pepper mix into the mushrooms, and top with feta.

PER SERVING

Calories: 116 | Total Fat: 6g | Protein: 7g | Carbs: 12g | Sugar: 6g | Fiber: 4g | Sodium: 126mg

Minestrone with Red Beans, Zucchini, and Spinach

Prep Time: 15 minutes | Cook Time: 45 minutes | Serves 8

- 2 tablespoons avocado oil
- 1 cup chopped onion
- 1 celery stalk, chopped
- 1 teaspoon dried thyme
- ½ teaspoon dried sage leaves
- ½ teaspoon freshly ground black pepper
- 2 cups Vegetable Broth or water
- 1 (28-ounce) carton or can chopped tomatoes
- 1 (15-ounce can) small red beans, rinsed and drained
- 2 carrots, peeled and chopped
- 2 bay leaves
- ½ cup whole wheat orzo, uncooked (optional)
- 1 medium zucchini, quartered lengthwise, then chopped
- 2 cups baby spinach
- ¼ cup freshly grated Parmesan cheese
- Chopped fresh basil (optional)

1. Set the electric pressure cooker to the Sauté setting. When the pot is hot, pour in the avocado oil.
2. Sauté the onion and celery for 3 to 5 minutes, or until the vegetables begin to soften. Stir in the thyme, sage, and pepper. Hit Cancel.
3. Add the broth, tomatoes and their juices, beans, carrots, bay leaves, and orzo (if using).
4. Close and lock the lid of the pressure cooker. Set the valve to sealing.
5. Cook on high pressure for 5 minutes.
6. When the cooking is complete, hit Cancel and quick release the pressure.
7. Once the pin drops, unlock and remove the lid.
8. 1.Stir in the zucchini and spinach. Replace the lid and let the pot sit for 10 minutes.
9. 2.Spoon into serving bowls and top with the Parmesan cheese and basil (if using).

PER SERVING

Calories: 152 | Total Fat: 5g | Protein: 6g | Carbs: 23g | Sugar: 8g | Fiber: 7g | Sodium: 357mg

Salt-Free Chickpeas

Prep Time: 5 minutes | Cook Time: 1 hour | Serves 6

- 1 pound dried chickpeas
- 2 bay leaves
- Fresh herbs, like parsley, thyme, rosemary, etc., cut into 3-inch pieces and tied together with kitchen twine (optional)

1. Rinse the chickpeas and put them in the electric pressure cooker. Add 8 cups of water, the bay leaves, and the herbs (if using).
2. Close and lock the lid. Turn the pressure valve to sealing.
3. Cook on high pressure for 35 minutes.
4. When the cooking is complete, hit Cancel. Allow the pressure to release naturally for 20 minutes, then quick release any remaining pressure.
5. Unlock and remove the lid. Discard the bay leaves and herb bundle.
6. Transfer the chickpeas to storage containers, covered with the cooking liquid, and let cool. Refrigerate for 3 or 4 days or freeze for up to 6 months.

PER SERVING

Calories: 138 | Total Fat: 2g | Protein: 8g | Carbs: 23g | Sugar: 4g | Fiber: 7g | Sodium: 0mg

Chapter 9
Desserts

Blackberry Yogurt Ice Pops

Prep Time: 10 minutes, plus 6 hours to freeze | Cook Time: 0 minutes | Serves 4

- 12 ounces plain Greek yogurt
- 1 cup blackberries
- Pinch nutmeg
- ¼ cup milk
- 2 (1-gram) packets stevia

1. In a blender, combine all of the ingredients. Blend until smooth.
2. Pour the mixture into 4 ice pop molds. Freeze for 6 hours before serving.

PER SERVING

Calories: 75 | Total Fat: 6g | Saturated Fat: 0g | Sodium: 7mg | Carbs: 9g | Fiber: 2g | Protein: 9g

Coffee And Cream Pops

Prep Time: 10 minutes, plus 6 hours to freeze | Cook Time: 5 minutes | Serves 4

- 2 teaspoons espresso powder (or to taste)
- 2 cups canned coconut milk
- ½ teaspoon vanilla extract
- ½ teaspoon cinnamon
- 3 (1-gram) packets stevia

1. In a medium saucepan over medium-low heat, heat all of the ingredients, stirring constantly, until the espresso powder is completely dissolved, about 5 minutes.
2. Pour the mixture into 4 ice pop molds. Freeze for 6 hours before serving.

PER SERVING

Calories: 225 | Total Fat: 24g | Saturated Fat: 21g | Sodium: 15mg | Carbs: 7g | Fiber: 3g | Protein: 2g

Frozen Apricot Mousse

Prep Time: 10 minutes | Cook Time: 0 minutes | Serves 2-4

- 1 cup of apricot apple butter
- 1/2 cup of whipping cream
- 2 egg whites
- 2 tablespoons of Fruit Sweet

1. Beat egg whites until stiff.
2. Stir in apricot apple butter.
3. Whip the cream to stiff peaks, adding the Fruit Sweet.
4. Add whipped cream into the apricot mixture. Freeze. Serve and enjoy

PER SERVING

Calories: 375 | Protein: 3g | Carbs: 41g | Dietary Fiber: 3g | Sugar: 11g | Fat: 23g

Oatmeal-Cranberry Cookies

Prep Time: 15 minutes | Cook Time: 10 minutes | Serves 18 cookies

- ½ cup melted butter
- ¼ cup honey
- 1 large egg
- 1 teaspoon pure vanilla extract
- 1 cup white whole-wheat flour
- 1 cup rolled oats
- 1 cup leftover cooked quinoa
- ½ cup dried cranberries
- ½ teaspoon baking soda
- ¼ teaspoon baking powder
- ¼ teaspoon ground nutmeg
- ¼ teaspoon sea salt
- ⅛ teaspoon ground allspice

1. Preheat the oven to 375°F. Line a baking sheet with parchment paper.
2. In a large bowl, mix the butter, honey, egg, and vanilla.
3. In a medium bowl, stir the flour, oats, quinoa, cranberries, baking soda, baking powder, nutmeg, salt, and allspice until well combined.
4. Add the dry ingredients to the wet ingredients and stir until combined.
5. Scoop the batter in heaped tablespoons onto the baking sheet and flatten out.
6. Bake for 10 minutes, or until golden brown.
7. Store the cookies in a sealed container at room temperature for 5 days or freeze for up to 1 month.

PER SERVING

Calories: 127 | Total Fat: 6g | Saturated Fat: 3g | Sodium: 98mg | Carbs: 16g | Sugar: 6g | Fiber: 2g | Protein: 2g

Raspberry Mousse

Prep Time: 20 minutes | Cook Time: 0 minutes | Serves 2-4

- 2/3 cup of Strawberry Fanciful
- 1/8 teaspoon of cream of tartar
- 2 egg whites
- 1/2 cup of whipping cream

1. Add cream of tartar to egg whites, beat until stiff.
2. Fold in Strawberry Fanciful.
3. Fold whipped cream into fruit mixture. Chill before serving.
4. For a flavor variation, try blueberry, strawberry, orange pineapple, berry pineapple, or peach.
5. Serve and enjoy!

PER SERVING

Calories: 260 | Protein: 2g | Carbs: 29g | Dietary Fiber: 0.5g | Sugar: 10g | Fat: 14g

Ginger Cake with Caramel-Apple Topping

Prep Time: 15 minutes | **Cook Time:** 45 minutes | **Serves** 15

- 2 cups harvest peach or vanilla fat-free yogurt
- 1⁄2 cup caramel fat-free topping
- 1 1⁄4 cups whole wheat flour
- 1 cup all-purpose flour
- 1⁄4 cup sugar
- 1 teaspoon baking soda
- 1 teaspoon ground cinnamon
- 1 teaspoon ground ginger
- 1⁄2 teaspoon salt
- 1⁄2 cup molasses
- 1⁄3 cup canola oil
- 1 egg
- 1 medium tart apple, chopped
- Lemon juice

1. Heat oven to 350°F. Grease and flour 9-inch square pan. In medium bowl, mix 3⁄4 cup of the yogurt and the caramel topping | cover and refrigerate until serving time.
2. In large bowl, beat remaining 1 1⁄4 cups yogurt and all remaining ingredients except apple and lemon juice with electric mixer on low speed 45 seconds, scraping bowl constantly. Beat on medium speed 1 minute, scraping bowl occasionally, until well blended. Stir in half of the chopped apple. Pour batter into pan. Sprinkle lemon juice over remaining apple | cover and refrigerate until serving time.
3. Bake 38 to 43 minutes or until toothpick inserted in center comes out clean. Cool slightly. Serve with topping mixture and remaining chopped apple.

PER SERVING

Calories: 230 | Total Fat: 6g | Cholesterol: 15mg | Sodium: 220mg | Total Carbs: 40g | Protein: 3g

Creamy Key Lime Pie

Prep Time: 30 minutes | **Cook Time:** 3 hours | **Serves** 8

- 2 cups Fiber One® cereal
- 1⁄4 cup butter or margarine, melted
- 1 tablespoon corn syrup
- 1 teaspoon vanilla
- 2 tablespoons cold water
- 1 tablespoon lime juice
- 1 1⁄2 teaspoons unflavored gelatin
- 4 oz (half of 8-oz package) 1⁄3-less-fat cream cheese (Neufchâtel), softened
- 3 containers (6 oz each) Key lime pie low-fat yogurt
- 1⁄2 cup frozen (thawed) reduced-fat whipped topping
- 2 teaspoons grated lime peel

1. Heat oven to 350°F. Place cereal in resealable food-storage plastic bag | seal bag and finely crush with rolling pin or meat mallet until cereal looks like graham cracker crumbs (or finely crush in food processor).
2. In medium bowl, mix crust ingredients until blended. Press crust mixture evenly and firmly in bottom and up side of ungreased 9-inch glass pie plate. Bake 10 to 12 minutes or until firm. Cool completely, about 1 hour.
3. In 1-quart saucepan, mix water and lime juice. Sprinkle gelatin on lime juice mixture | let stand 1 minute. Heat over low heat, stirring constantly, until gelatin is dissolved. Cool slightly, about 2 minutes.
4. In medium bowl, beat cream cheese with electric mixer on medium speed until smooth. Add yogurt and lime juice mixture | beat on low speed until well blended. Fold in whipped topping and lime peel. Spoon into crust. Refrigerate until set, about 2 hours.

PER SERVING

Calories: 210 | Total Fat: 10g | Cholesterol: 25mg | Sodium: 180mg | Total Carbs: 24g | Protein: 4g

Tzatziki Sauce

Prep Time: 15 minutes | **Cook Time:** 0 minutes | **Serves** 1½ cups

- 1 cup low-fat plain Greek yogurt
- ½ English cucumber, grated, with all the liquid squeezed out
- Juice of ½ lemon
- 1 tablespoon chopped fresh dill
- 1 teaspoon minced garlic
- Sea salt
- Freshly ground black pepper

1. In a small bowl, stir together the yogurt, cucumber, lemon juice, dill, and garlic until well blended.
2. Season with salt and pepper. Refrigerate the sauce in a sealed container for up to 5 days.

PER SERVING

Calories: 31 | Total Fat: 1g | Saturated Fat: 0g | Sodium: 55mg | Carbs: 4g | Sugar: 3g | Fiber: 1g | Protein: 2g

Fruit Dip

Prep Time: 5 minutes | **Cook Time:** 5 minutes | **Serves** 1

- 1 cup of plain yogurt
- 8 ounces of light cream
- 1 tablespoon Equal sugar
- 1 teaspoon of vanilla.

1. Mix all of the ingredients together.
2. Serve and enjoy!

PER SERVING

Calories: 117.7 | Protein: 1.5g | Carbs: 13.4g | Sugar: 7.7g | Fat: 6.6g | Saturated Fat: 4.1g | Cholesterol: 20.5mg

Dark Chocolate Cupcakes

Prep Time: 35 minutes | Cook Time: 35 minutes | Serves 12

- 1½ oz bittersweet baking chocolate (3 squares from 4-oz bar), finely chopped
- 6 tablespoons unsweetened dark baking cocoa
- ½ teaspoon instant espresso coffee powder
- ½ cup fat-free (skim) milk
- ¾ cup white whole wheat flour
- ¾ teaspoon baking soda
- ¼ teaspoon salt
- ¼ cup fat-free egg product
- ½ cup granulated sugar
- ¼ cup packed brown sugar
- 3 tablespoons canola oil
- 2 teaspoons vanilla
- 2 teaspoons fat-free (skim) milk
- 1 tablespoon unsweetened dark baking cocoa
- 1 oz fat-free cream cheese (from 8-oz package)
- ⅓ cup powdered sugar
- ⅛ teaspoon vanilla
- Pinch salt
- ¼ oz bittersweet baking chocolate (½ square from 4-oz bar), grated

1. Heat oven to 350°F. Place paper baking cup in each of 12 regular-size muffin cups.
2. In small bowl, add chocolate, cocoa and espresso powder. In small microwavable measuring cup, microwave milk uncovered on High 30 seconds or until steaming but not boiling. Pour over chocolate mixture | stir. Cover | let stand 5 minutes. Stir until smooth.
3. Meanwhile, in medium bowl, stir flour, baking soda and salt. In large bowl, beat egg product with electric mixer on medium speed 30 seconds. Gradually add Sugar:, about ¼ cup at a time, beating well after each addition. Beat 2 minutes longer. Beat in oil and vanilla. Beat about ⅓ of the flour mixture and about ½ of the chocolate mixture at a time alternately into sugar mixture on low speed until blended.
4. Divide batter evenly among muffin cups, filling each about ⅔ full. Bake 20 to 25 minutes or until tops spring back when touched lightly in center. Cool 5 minutes | transfer from muffin cups to cooling rack. Cool completely before glazing.
5. In small bowl or microwavable custard cup, heat milk uncovered on High about 10 seconds or until hot. Stir in cocoa until smooth.
6. In separate small bowl, stir cream cheese until smooth. Stir in cocoa mixture until blended. Stir in powdered sugar. Stir in vanilla and salt until mixture is smooth and shiny. Spoon about 1 teaspoon glaze over each cupcake | spread to edge with back of spoon. Sprinkle about ¼ teaspoon grated chocolate over each glazed cupcake.

PER SERVING

Calories: 170 | Total Fat: 6g | Cholesterol: 0mg | Sodium: 190mg | Total Carbs: 27g | Protein: 3g

Fudge Sweet Brownies

Prep Time: 15 minutes | Cook Time: 0minutes | Serves 2-4

- 2/3 cup of flour
- 1/2 teaspoon of baking powder
- 2 eggs, beaten well
- 1/2 cup of melted butter or oil
- 1/2 cup of Fudge Sweet, softened
- 1/2 cup of Fruit Sweet
- 1 teaspoon of vanilla
- 1/2 cup of walnuts, chopped

1. Sift in baking powder and flour | set aside.
2. Stir in butter or oil, eggs, Fudge Sweet, Fruit Sweet, and vanilla.
3. Add flour mixture and mix without allowing lumps to form. Add the walnuts.
4. Pour the mixture into a greased and floured baking dish.
5. Bake at 350 degrees for about 15 mins, until the cake springs back at a light touch.
6. The doubled recipe will fit into a double size cookie pan.
7. Serve and enjoy!

PER SERVING

Calories: 200 | Protein: 5g | Carbs: 39g | Dietary Fiber: 2g | Sugar: 8g | Fat: 12.5g

Everyday Balsamic Vinaigrette

Prep Time: 10 minutes | Cook Time: 0 minutes | Serves ¾ cup

- ½ cup extra-virgin olive oil
- ¼ cup balsamic vinegar
- 2 teaspoons chopped fresh oregano
- 1 teaspoon Dijon mustard
- 1 teaspoon chopped fresh thyme
- Sea salt
- Freshly ground black pepper

1. In a small bowl, whisk together the oil, vinegar, oregano, mustard, and thyme until well blended.
2. Season the dressing with salt and pepper. Store in a sealed container at room temperature for up to 1 week.

PER SERVING

Calories: 170 | Total Fat: 18g | Saturated Fat: 2g | Sodium: 38mg | Carbs: 2g | Sugar: 2g | Fiber: 0g | Protein: 0g

Brownie Torte

Prep Time: 20 minutes | Cook Time: 0 minutes | Serves 30 cookies

- 1 1/2 cup of chilled whipping cream
- 3 tablespoon of Fruit Sweet or to taste
- 1 teaspoon of vanilla

1. Prepare Fudge Sweet Brownies
2. Whip up the Fruit Sweet, cream, and vanilla and use as a filling and topping for the layers of brownies.
3. About 3 cups frozen whipped topping, thawed.
4. Replace the vanilla with your favorite flavors, such as 1 tablespoon of orange juice concentrate or 1 tablespoon of instant coffee.
5. Serve and enjoy!

PER SERVING

Calories: 483 | Protein: 6.2g | Carbs: 62g | Dietary Fiber: 3g | Sugar: 1.7g | Fat: 27g

Buffalo Bites

Prep Time: 5 minutes | Cook Time: 10 minutes | Serves 4

- 1 egg
- ½ head of cauliflower, separated into florets
- 1 cup panko bread crumbs
- 1 cup low-fat ranch dressing
- ½ cup hot sauce
- ½ tsp salt
- ½ tsp garlic powder
- Black pepper
- Nonstick cooking spray

1. Heat oven to 400 degrees. Spray a baking sheet with cooking spray.
2. Place the egg in a medium bowl and mix in the salt, pepper and garlic. Place the panko crumbs into a small bowl.
3. Dip the florets first in the egg then into the panko crumbs. Place in a single layer on prepared pan.
4. Bake 8-10 minutes, stirring halfway through, until cauliflower is golden brown and crisp on the outside.
5. In a small bowl stir the dressing and hot sauce together. Use for dipping.

PER SERVING

Calories: 132 | Total Carbs: 15g | Net Carbs: 14g | Protein: 6g | Fat 5g | Sugar 4g | Fiber: 1g

Candied Pecans

Prep Time: 5 minutes | Cook Time: 10 minutes | Serves 6

- 1 ½ tsp butter
- 1 ½ cup pecan halves
- 2 ½ tbsp. Splenda, divided
- 1 tsp cinnamon
- ¼ tsp ginger
- 1/8 tsp cardamom
- 1/8 tsp salt

1. In a small bowl, stir together 1 1/2 teaspoons Splenda, cinnamon, ginger, cardamom and salt. Set aside.
2. Melt butter in a medium skillet over med-low heat. Add pecans, and two tablespoons Splenda. Reduce heat to low and cook, stirring occasionally, until sweetener melts, about 5 to 8 minutes.
3. Add spice mixture to the skillet and stir to coat pecans. Spread mixture to parchment paper and let cool for 10-15 minutes. Store in an airtight container. Serving size is ¼ cup.

PER SERVING

Calories: 173 | Total Carbs: 8g | Net Carbs: 6g | Protein: 2g | Fat 16g | Sugar: 6g | Fiber: 2g

Blackberry Soufflés

Prep Time: 15 minutes | Cook Time: 30 minutes | Serves 4

- 12 oz. blackberries
- 4 egg whites
- 1/3 cup Splenda
- 1 tbsp. water
- 1 tbsp. Swerve powdered sugar
- Nonstick cooking spray

1. Heat oven to 375 degrees. Spray 4 1-cup ramekins with cooking spray.
2. In a small saucepan, over med-high heat, combine blackberries and 1 tablespoon water, bring to a boil. Reduce heat and simmer until berries are soft. Add Splenda and stir over medium heat until Splenda dissolves, without boiling.
3. Bring back to boiling, reduce heat and simmer 5 minutes. Remove from heat and cool 5 minutes.
4. Place a fine meshed sieve over a small bowl and push the berry mixture through it using the back of a spoon. Discard the seeds. Cover and chill 15 minutes.
5. In a large bowl, beat egg whites until soft peaks form. Gently fold in berry mixture. Spoon evenly into prepared ramekins and place them on a baking sheet.
6. Bake 12 minutes, or until puffed and light brown. Dust with powdered Swerve and serve immediately.

PER SERVING

Calories: 141 | Total Carbs: 26g | Net Carbs: 21g | Protein: 5g | Fat 0g | Sugar: 20g | Fiber: 5g

Appendix 1 Measurement Conversion Chart

Volume Equivalents (Dry)

US STANDARD	METRIC (APPROXIMATE)
1/8 teaspoon	0.5 mL
1/4 teaspoon	1 mL
1/2 teaspoon	2 mL
3/4 teaspoon	4 mL
1 teaspoon	5 mL
1 tablespoon	15 mL
1/4 cup	59 mL
1/2 cup	118 mL
3/4 cup	177 mL
1 cup	235 mL
2 cups	475 mL
3 cups	700 mL
4 cups	1 L

Volume Equivalents (Liquid)

US STANDARD	US STANDARD (OUNCES)	METRIC (APPROXIMATE)
2 tablespoons	1 fl.oz.	30 mL
1/4 cup	2 fl.oz.	60 mL
1/2 cup	4 fl.oz.	120 mL
1 cup	8 fl.oz.	240 mL
1 1/2 cup	12 fl.oz.	355 mL
2 cups or 1 pint	16 fl.oz.	475 mL
4 cups or 1 quart	32 fl.oz.	1 L
1 gallon	128 fl.oz.	4 L

Weight Equivalents

US STANDARD	METRIC (APPROXIMATE)
1 ounce	28 g
2 ounces	57 g
5 ounces	142 g
10 ounces	284 g
15 ounces	425 g
16 ounces (1 pound)	455 g
1.5 pounds	680 g
2 pounds	907 g

Temperatures Equivalents

FAHRENHEIT(F)	CELSIUS(C) APPROXIMATE
225 °F	107 °C
250 °F	120 ° °C
275 °F	135 °C
300 °F	150 °C
325 °F	160 °C
350 °F	180 °C
375 °F	190 °C
400 °F	205 °C
425 °F	220 °C
450 °F	235 °C
475 °F	245 °C
500 °F	260 °C

Appendix 2 The Dirty Dozen and Clean Fifteen

The Environmental Working Group (EWG) is a nonprofit, nonpartisan organization dedicated to protecting human health and the environment Its mission is to empower people to live healthier lives in a healthier environment. This organization publishes an annual list of the twelve kinds of produce, in sequence, that have the highest amount of pesticide residue-the Dirty Dozen-as well as a list of the fifteen kinds of produce that have the least amount of pesticide residue-the Clean Fifteen.

THE DIRTY DOZEN	
The 2016 Dirty Dozen includes the following produce. These are considered among the year's most important produce to buy organic:	
Strawberries	Spinach
Apples	Tomatoes
Nectarines	Bell peppers
Peaches	Cherry tomatoes
Celery	Cucumbers
Grapes	Kale/collard greens
Cherries	Hot peppers

The Dirty Dozen list contains two additional itemskale/collard greens and hot peppers-because they tend to contain trace levels of highly hazardous pesticides.

THE CLEAN FIFTEEN	
The least critical to buy organically are the Clean Fifteen list. The following are on the 2016 list:	
Avocados	Papayas
Corn	Kiw
Pineapples	Eggplant
Cabbage	Honeydew
Sweet peas	Grapefruit
Onions	Cantaloupe
Asparagus	Cauliflower
Mangos	

Some of the sweet corn sold in the United States are made from genetically engineered (GE) seedstock. Buy organic varieties of these crops to avoid GE produce.

Appendix 3 Index

AMELIE HORTON

Printed in Great Britain
by Amazon

16995708R00045